Number
Journey

for ages 7-8

A & C Black • London

Andrew Brodie: Number Journey for ages 7-8 © A&C Black Publishers Ltd 2008

Contents

Andrew Brodie: Number Journey for ages 7-8 © A&C Black Publishers Ltd 2008

Introduction

Number Journey has been specially written to help teachers ensure progression in the teaching of number by addressing two key areas: the involvement of parents and the use of day-to-day assessment to promote success.

For many parents, the current methods used for teaching mathematics can be something of a mystery. Parents recognise certain aspects from their own school days but are surprised by some of the other approaches that are now being used in schools. The clash between the methods with which the parents are familiar and the methods their children are using in school can lead to many frustrations at home. The Williams review of 'Mathematics Teaching in Early Years Settings and Primary Schools' emphasises the role that parents can play in helping their children to learn mathematics. This can be summarised in the following four statements:

- Parents should be at the centre of any plan to improve children's outcomes.

- The panel heard time and again from children that they would like their parents to be taught the methods they are learning in mathematics, which have changed considerably since their parents were at school.

- The panel believes that the lack of clarification and setting out of the methods of teaching is a missed opportunity for engaging parents and improving their children's attainment.

- There is an opportunity for schools to work together with parents to dispel myths about the mystery of mathematics and give both children and parents a good grounding and positive attitude to this subject.

Number Journey addresses all four statements by providing materials that schools can use to ensure parents are given the opportunity to take an active part in their children's mathematical education. Current methods are explained clearly and the explanations are accompanied by activities that can be used at home to provide positive support for work at school. The teachers' notes for each unit specify clear learning objectives and list both outcomes and success criteria to enable teachers to make reliable assessments of pupils' work. The worksheets themselves are used to determine whether pupils have met the success criteria.

3

How is the book organised?

The materials in this book are organised into 15 units all designed to address the teaching of number – an area of maths in which many parents feel least confident but where they can actually be most helpful. *The Framework for mathematics teaching* includes a very wide range of learning objectives for understanding number, using number facts and calculating. In this book we have focused on the objectives where parental involvement will be most effective.

Each unit features an introductory page for teachers (*Teacher's Notes*), a letter for parents (*Help at Home Sheet*) that can be photocopied and sent home and two pupil worksheets (*Worksheets 1 and 2*). The calculation methods demonstrated on all the sheets are based on those recommended by the National Strategy.

Teacher's notes

These notes specify the learning objectives, learning outcomes and success criteria for each unit as well as suggesting opportunities for using and applying the skill being practised. The questions listed under 'Success criteria' are intended as prompts on which to base ongoing pupil assessment.

Help at home sheet

This is a letter for parents explaining what is being taught and, where appropriate, it also shows worked examples for parents to follow. There are also some ideas for relevant activities that can be completed at home. Introducing maths into everyday situations can increase a child's confidence and they can end up tackling complex number operations without even realising they are 'doing maths'.

Worksheets 1 and 2

The two worksheets provide activities that can be used by pupils for learning, for practising and for assessment. Where possible the children are encouraged to participate in their own assessment, identifying what they can do. Once a sheet is completed, discuss it with the child and help them to think about their own learning process. Ask questions such as 'How did you get on? Did you like this work? Did you find any of it too challenging?' With the second worksheet, discuss with the child whether they feel able to tick the 'I can' boxes. Celebrate their successes and support them if they are not ready to tick the boxes yet, by explaining that they will have another chance to revisit the concept and get more practice until they feel more confident.

Andrew Brodie: Number Journey for ages 7-8 © A&C Black Publishers Ltd 2008

Reading, writing and ordering whole numbers to at least 1000

Teacher's notes

Building on previous learning
Before starting this unit check that the children can already:
- read and write two-digit and three-digit numbers in figures and words
- explain what each digit in a two-digit number represents, including numbers where 0 is a place holder
- order two-digit numbers and position them on a number line.

Learning objectives
- Read whole numbers to at least 1000.
- Write whole numbers to at least 1000.
- Position whole numbers to at least 1000 on a number line.

Learning outcomes
The children will be able to:
- read numbers to at least 1000, including those where 0 is a place holder.
- write numbers to at least 1000, including those where 0 is a place holder.
- write numbers, to at least 1000, in order.

Success criteria
Can the children…
… write clearly in figures the following numbers: seven hundred and twenty-five, nine hundred and three, eight hundred and eighty-eight, one hundred and six?
… write clearly in words the following numbers: 492, 309, 816, 344?
… write the following numbers in the correct order on a number line: 219, 402, 596, 834, 120, 650, 325, 775, 925?

Resources needed
- A class number line from 0 to 1000, marked at every multiple of 10. Ideally this should be stuck to the walls at ceiling height and will provide opportunities for discussion.

Opportunities for using and applying the skills
- Measuring in centimetres, beyond one metre.
- Finding specified pages in a large book.
- Changing money in pounds to pence e.g. 'How many pennies are there in £4.63?'

Andrew Brodie: Number Journey for ages 7-8 © A&C Black Publishers Ltd 2008

Reading, writing and ordering whole numbers to at least 1000

Help at home sheet

Child's name: **Date:**

Dear Parents

At school we follow the National Curriculum and the Primary Framework for mathematics. One aspect of our work in mathematics is the learning of number skills and part of that is reading and writing whole numbers to at least 1000 and placing them in order. We are keen to involve parents in their children's learning so you may like to help your child by using some of the ideas on this sheet.

National Curriculum

The Primary Framework for mathematics says that Year 3 pupils should:
• read, write and order whole numbers to at least 1000 and position them on a number line.

You could...

... take the opportunity to count beyond 100 with your child whenever appropriate, for example when walking to school.

... play the book page game:

The challenge is to find page 746 in a dictionary of at least 1000 pages. Encourage your child to open the book at random and ask the following questions: "What page have you found? Can you read the number correctly? Do you need to go higher or lower to reach page 746? Turn over a set of pages to get closer to 746 – what page have you found? Do you need to go higher or lower this time?" Keep playing until the correct page is reached then ask your child to set you a page to find, all the time practising reading the numbers as well as learning which numbers are higher or lower than others.

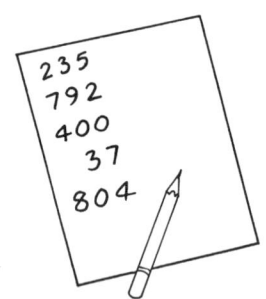

... dictate numbers for your child to write. Give him/her a piece of paper and a pencil and ask him/her to write the following numbers: 235, 792, 400, 37, 804, 999, 1000. Watch out for any mistakes and try to work out why he/she might have made them so that you can give some tips on how the numbers should be written. Give plenty of encouragement and praise.

0 1 2 3 4 5 6 7 8 9

You may like to let us know how your child gets on with these activities – if so please return this sheet with any comments on the back.

Andrew Brodie: Number Journey for ages 7-8 © A&C Black Publishers Ltd 2008

Reading, writing and ordering whole numbers to at least 1000

Worksheet 1

Name: _____

Date: _____

On this page I will be writing numbers in figures and words.

Match the numbers to the words. The first one has been done for you.

645	four hundred and seven
505	nine hundred and ninety-eight
13	two hundred and sixty-three
263	eighty-seven
407	five hundred and fifty
800	eight hundred
989	six hundred and forty-five
998	thirteen
87	nine hundred and eighty-nine
50	five hundred and five

Write these numbers in figures. The first one has been done for you.

three hundred and fourteen   314

seven hundred and twenty-five   _____

nine hundred and three   _____

eight hundred and eighty-eight   _____

Write these numbers in words. The first one has been done for you.

700   _____ seven hundred _____

492   _____

309   _____

816   _____

Andrew Brodie: Number Journey for ages 7-8 © A&C Black Publishers Ltd 2008

Reading, writing and ordering whole numbers to at least 1000

Worksheet 2

Name: _____

Date: _____

Look at these numbers: 219   402   596   834   120   650   325   775

Write each number with the correct arrow on the number line.

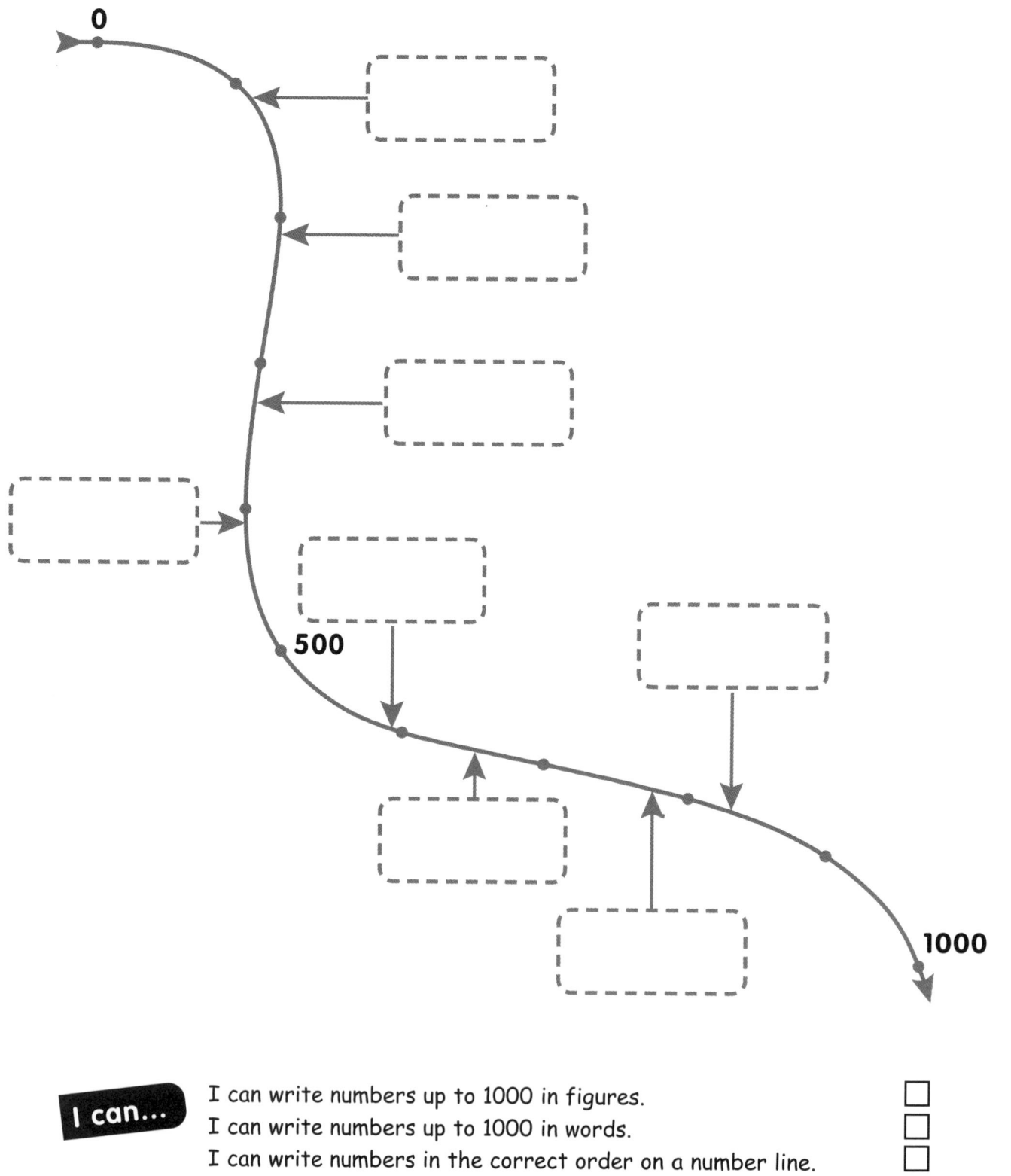

I can...

I can write numbers up to 1000 in figures. ☐

I can write numbers up to 1000 in words. ☐

I can write numbers in the correct order on a number line. ☐

Andrew Brodie: Number Journey for ages 7-8 © A&C Black Publishers Ltd 2008

Teacher's notes

Building on previous learning
Before starting this unit check that the children can already:
- read and write two-digit and three-digit numbers in figures and words
- recognise multiples of 10
- describe and extend number sequences

Learning objectives
- Count on from zero in single-digit steps.
- Count back to zero in single-digit steps.
- Count on from zero in multiples of 10.
- Count back to zero in multiples of 10.

Learning outcomes
The children will be able to:
- count on from zero in tens, twos or fives to 100 and beyond; in threes to at least 30, in fours to at least 40, in sixes to at least sixty, in sevens to at least 70, in eights to at least 80 and in nines to at least 90.
- count back to zero from the numbers listed above and in the steps listed above.
- count on from zero in fifties or hundreds to at least 1000; in twenties to at least 200, in thirties to at least 300, in forties to at least 400, in sixties to at least 600, in seventies to at least 700, in eighties to at least 800 and in nineties to at least 900.
- count back to zero from the numbers listed above and in the steps listed above.

Success criteria
Can the children…
…continue sequences by counting on in fours, tens, fives, sixes or twenties?
…continue sequences by counting back in twos, fives, fours, fifties or nines?

Resources needed
- A class number line from 0 to 1000, marked at every multiple of 10 – ideally this can be stuck to the wall at ceiling height. You could use this every day for a few minutes at the start of your maths lesson, one day counting on from zero in fifties and showing the 'jumps' by pointing with a stick to the number line, another day counting on in seventies, etc.

Opportunities for using and applying the skills
- Identifying patterns and relationships involving numbers.
- Making measurements in steps of specified numbers of centimetres e.g. measuring the length of a PE bench in steps of 40cm because a 40cm length of string is easy for pupils to hold.

Counting on from or back to zero in single-digit steps or multiples of 10

Help at home sheet

Child's name: **Date:**

Dear Parents

At school we follow the National Curriculum and the Primary Framework for mathematics. One aspect of our work in mathematics is the learning of number skills and part of that concerns counting in twos, fives or other single-digit steps. To be able to do this the children need to understand the relationship between numbers as shown on a number line. We are keen to involve parents in their children's learning so you may like to help your child by using some of the ideas on this sheet.

National Curriculum

The Primary Framework for mathematics says that Year 3 pupils should:
• count on from and back to zero in single-digit steps or multiples of ten.

You could...

... draw a number line like this on a large sheet of paper ensuring it goes from 0 to 100:

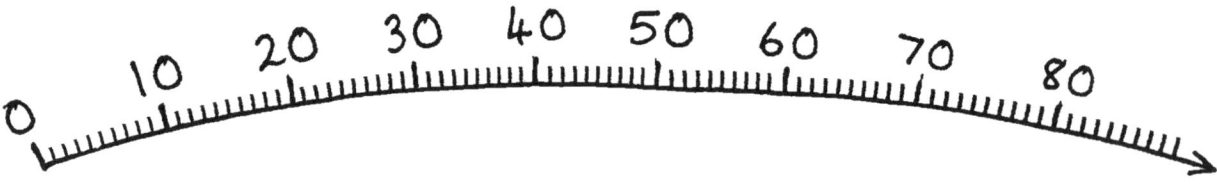

... then spend just five minutes a day practising counting on with your child e.g. one day you could count on in twos from 0 to 100, pointing out the 'jumps' on the number line. The next day you could count on in fives from 0 to 100. The next day you could count on in fours from 0 to 40 but this is harder to do. Help your child by encouraging him/her to point at the correct numbers on the number line when counting, then stressing the number that is reached e.g. if counting in fours, start at 0, count 1, 2, 3, 4, gets us to 4, count 1, 2, 3, 4, gets us to 8, count 1, 2, 3, 4, gets us to 12, etc.

... use several pieces of paper to draw your number line so that you can have a straight number line that can be fastened along a wall.

You may like to let us know how your child gets on with these activities – if so please return this sheet with any comments on the back.

Andrew Brodie: Number Journey for ages 7-8 © A&C Black Publishers Ltd 2008

Worksheet 1

Name: _____

Date: _____

On this page I will be counting on to make number sequences.

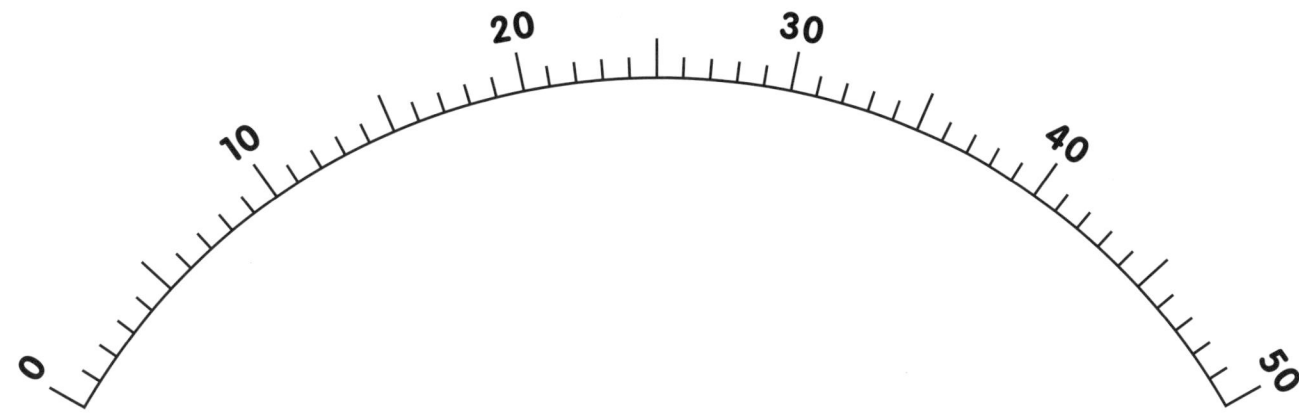

Look at this number sequence.

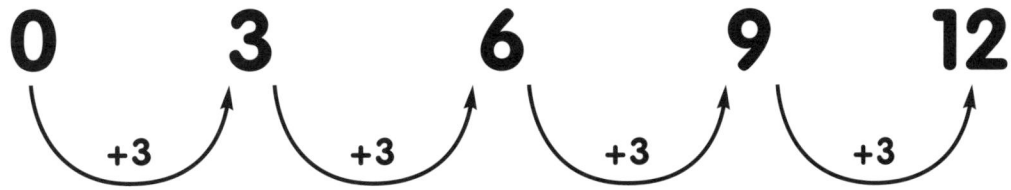

Write the next 3 numbers for each of these number sequences.

0, 4, 8, 12, 16, 20,

0, 10, 20, 30,

0, 5, 10, 15, 20, 25,

0, 6, 12, 18, 24, 30,

0, 20, 40, 60,

Andrew Brodie: Number Journey for ages 7-8 © A&C Black Publishers Ltd 2008

Worksheet 2

Name: _____

Date: _____

20   **30**

0   10   20   30   40   50

Look at this number sequence.

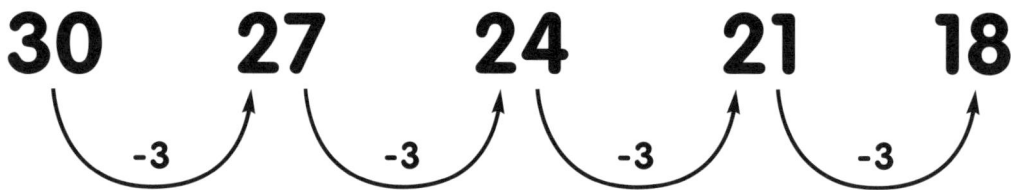

30   **27**   **24**   **21**   **18**

-3   -3   -3   -3

Write the next 3 numbers for each of these number sequences.

20, 18, 16, 14, 12, 10,   ☐ , ☐ , ☐ , …

50, 45, 40, 35, 30, 25,   ☐ , ☐ , ☐ , …

40, 36, 32, 28, 24, 20,   ☐ , ☐ , ☐ , …

500, 450, 400, 350, 300, 250,   ☐ , ☐ , ☐ , …

90, 81, 72, 63, 54, 45,   ☐ , ☐ , ☐ , …

I can...   I can count on from zero in single-digit steps.   ☐
I can count back to zero in single-digit steps.   ☐
I can count on from zero in twenties.   ☐
I can count back to zero in fifties.   ☐

12

Andrew Brodie: Number Journey for ages 7-8 © A&C Black Publishers Ltd 2008

Partitioning three-digit numbers into multiples of 100, 10 and 1

Teacher's notes

Building on previous learning
Before starting this unit check that the children can already:
- read and write two-digit numbers and three-digit numbers in figures and words
- partition two-digit numbers in different ways, including into multiples of 10 and 1.

Learning objectives
- Partition three-digit numbers into multiples of 100, 10 and 1 in different ways.

Learning outcomes
The children will be able to:
- know what each digit in a three-digit number represents.
- recognise 0 as a place holder in three-digit numbers such as 907 and 240.
- partition numbers such as 462 into 400 + 60 + 2.
- calculate the values of unknown numbers in number sentences such as 842 = 800 + ⬚ + 2

Success criteria
Can the children…

…write the missing numbers in the boxes: 452 = 400 + 50 + ⬚ ,
619 = 600 + ⬚ + 9, 874 = ⬚ + 70 + 4, 118 = 100 + ⬚ + 8?

…identify the single step that will change each of the first numbers into the second numbers in the following set of number pairs: 526, 726; 149, 649; 352, 952; 714, 784; 927, 957; 461, 467?

Resources needed
- Number 'paddles' for each child, showing a set of multiples of 100, a set of multiples of 10 and a set of multiples of 1.

Opportunities for using and applying the skills
- Identifying patterns and relationships involving numbers and using these to solve problems.
- Money, particularly in terms of amounts in excess of one hundred pounds e.g. solving problems such as: 'Mrs Brown has £432 in the bank then she takes out exactly £200. How much has she got left?' It's important that the children see the numbers, 432 and 200, so that they can observe that only the hundreds are affected. They could then consider questions such as: 'Mrs Brown has £584 in the bank then she takes out exactly £30. How much has she got left?' Again, they need to look at the numbers, 584 and 30, to observe that only the tens are affected.

Andrew Brodie: Number Journey for ages 7-8 © A&C Black Publishers Ltd 2008

Partitioning three-digit numbers into multiples of 100, 10 and 1

Help at home sheet

Child's name: **Date:**

Dear Parents

At school we follow the National Curriculum and the Primary Framework for mathematics. One aspect of our work in mathematics is the learning of number skills and part of that concerns partitioning a number such as 384 to show that it can be split into 3 hundreds, 8 tens and 4 units (note that some teachers may use the word 'ones' instead of 'units'). We are keen to involve parents in their children's learning so you may like to help your child by using some of the ideas on this sheet.

National Curriculum

The Primary Framework for mathematics says that Year 3 pupils should:
• partition three-digit numbers into multiples of 100, 10 and 1 in different ways.

You could...

… make some number cards as shown below. Make 9 cards of each size so that on the first set of cards you can write 100, 200, 300, 400, 500, 600, 700, 800, 900. On the second set of cards you can write 10, 20, 30, 40, 50, 60, 70, 80, 90. On the third set of cards you can write 1, 2, 3, 4, 5, 6, 7, 8, 9.

4	0	0

7	0

3

Once you have made the cards, pick one from the first set, one from the second set and one from the third set and place them on top of each other. The three shown above would make the number four hundred and seventy-three for example. Ask your child to read the number to you, then show him/her the 3 cards and ensure that he/she is able to identify the 3 numbers: four hundred, seventy and three. Now ask your child to pick one card from each set and to tell you what each one shows before he/she puts them together. Can he/she tell you what the finished number is? Keep practising and giving lots of encouragement and praise.

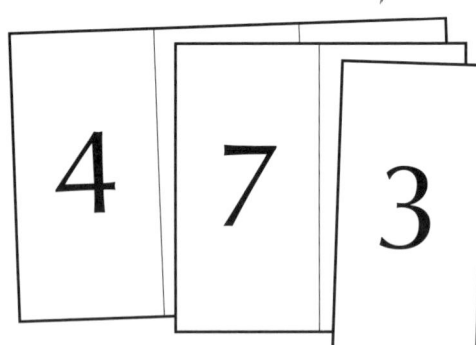

You may like to let us know how your child gets on with these activities – if so please return this sheet with any comments on the back.

Andrew Brodie: Number Journey for ages 7-8 © A&C Black Publishers Ltd 2008

Partitioning three-digit numbers into multiples of 100, 10 and 1

Worksheet 1

Name: _____

Date: _____

On this page I will be partitioning three-digit numbers.

Look at this number.

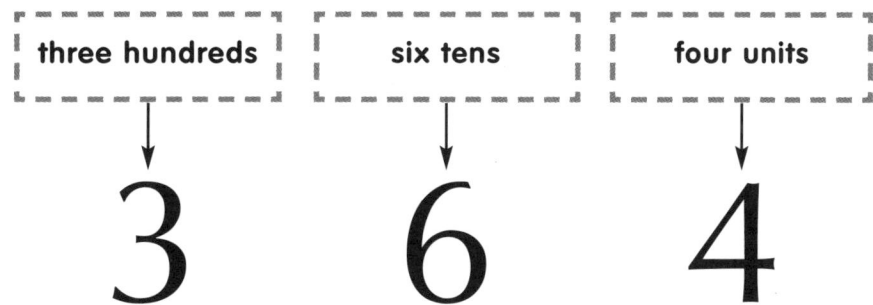

Label the digits on these numbers.

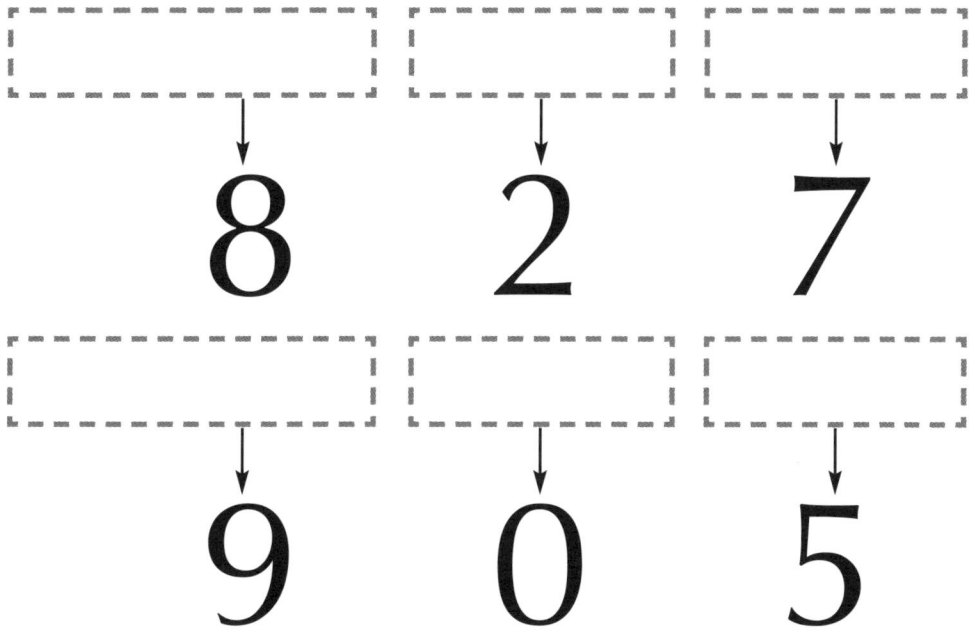

Write the number which has five hundreds, no tens and no units. ⬚

Write the number which has seven hundreds, three tens and eight units. ⬚

Write the number which has two hundreds, nine tens and no units. ⬚

Write the number which has six hundreds, five tens and six units. ⬚

Andrew Brodie: Number Journey for ages 7-8 © A&C Black Publishers Ltd 2008

Worksheet 2

Name: _____

Date: _____

Write the missing numbers in the boxes.

452 = 400 + 50 + ☐   619 = 600 + ☐ + 9

874 = ☐ + 70 + 4   118 = 100 + ☐ + 8

Look at this addition:

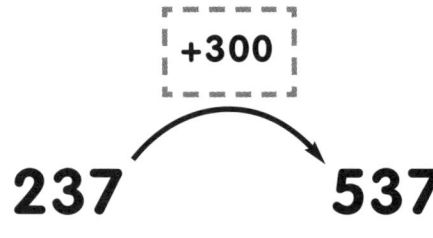

We started with 237. We added 300. We made 537. Only the hundreds changed. We still have 30 and we still have 7.

Write the correct numbers in the boxes.

| + |
526 → 726

| + |
714 → 784

| + |
149 → 649

| + |
927 → 957

| + |
352 → 952

| + |
461 → 467

 **I can...** I can partition three-digit numbers into multiples of 100, 10 and 1. ☐

Andrew Brodie: Number Journey for ages 7-8 © A&C Black Publishers Ltd 2008

Rounding two-digit or three-digit numbers to the nearest 10 or 100

Teacher's notes

Building on previous learning
Before starting this unit check that the children can already:
- read, write and order whole numbers to at least 1000 and position them on a number line.

Learning objectives
- Round two-digit numbers to the nearest 10.
- Round three-digit numbers to the nearest 10 or 100.

Learning outcomes
The children will be able to:
- round two-digit numbers to the nearest 10.
- round up numbers such as 65 to 70.
- round three digit numbers to the nearest 10 or 100.
- round up numbers such as 350 to 400.

Success criteria
Can the children…
…round the following numbers to the nearest 10: 11 17 22 26 33 35 375 425?
…round the following numbers to the nearest 100: 375 118 290 827 984 450?

Resources needed
- A class number line from 0 to 1000, marked at every multiple of 10. Ideally this can be stuck to the walls at ceiling height.

Opportunities for using and applying the skills
- Identifying patterns and relationships involving numbers and using these to solve problems.
- Estimating large numbers of items, e.g. the number of birds in a flock, the number of windows in an office block, the number of counters in a tray, etc.

Andrew Brodie: Number Journey for ages 7-8 © A&C Black Publishers Ltd 2008

Rounding two-digit or three-digit numbers to the nearest 10 or 100

Help at home sheet

Child's name:

Date:

Dear Parents

At school we follow the National Curriculum and the Primary Framework for mathematics. One aspect of our work in mathematics is the learning of number skills and part of that concerns rounding numbers to the nearest ten or to the nearest hundred. To be able to do this the children need to understand the relationship between numbers as shown on a number line. We are keen to involve parents in their children's learning so you may like to help your child by using some of the ideas on this sheet.

National Curriculum

The Primary Framework for mathematics says that Year 3 pupils should:
• round two-digit or three-digit numbers to the nearest 10 or 100.

You could...

...draw a number line like this on a large sheet of paper ensuring it goes from 0 to 100:

...write numbers such as 59, 17, 86, 91, 48, 32, 73 on small pieces of paper then ask your child to put them in the correct places on your number line. Your child could stick them in position with sticky tac. Talk about where the numbers are. Which multiple of ten is each number closest to? E.g. the number 59 is closest to 60. Encourage your child to say: "59 rounded to the nearest 10 is 60." Your child will make best progress with lots of practice and lots of praise. Now write numbers such as 25, 65, 85 and 35 on small pieces of paper and ask your child to put them in the correct places. Discuss the fact that 25 is exactly half way between 20 and 30 but that we always round up. Encourage your child to say: "25 rounded to the nearest 10 is 30."

...when your child is confident with the numbers less than 100, try higher numbers but without using a number line. Show him/her a number such as 482 and ask him/her to round it to the nearest 10. He/she should say, "482 to the nearest 10 is 480." Now ask him/her to round it to the nearest 100. Encourage him/her to realise that 482 is closer to 500 than 400.

As always give lots of practice, but just for a very short time each day, and lots of praise.

You may like to let us know how your child gets on with these activities – if so please return this sheet with any comments on the back.

Andrew Brodie: Number Journey for ages 7-8 © A&C Black Publishers Ltd 2008

Rounding two-digit or three-digit numbers to the nearest 10 or 100

Worksheet 1

Name: _____

Date: _____

On this page I will be rounding numbers to the nearest 10.

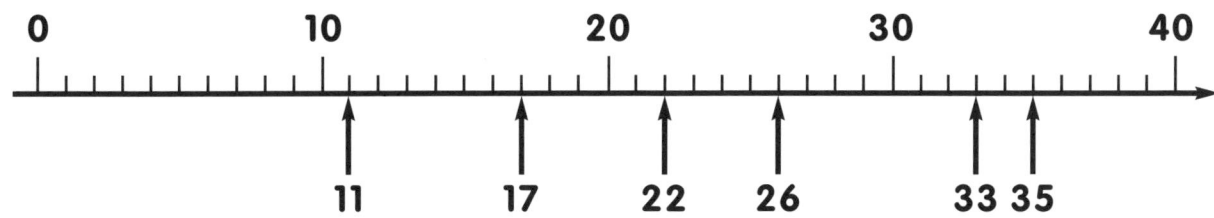

You can see that the number 26 is between 20 and 30. The numbers 20 and 30 are both multiples of 10. The number 26 is closer to 30 so...

... 26 —— to the nearest 10 ——→ **30**

Try these:

17 —— to the nearest 10 ——→ [ ]

11 —— to the nearest 10 ——→ [ ]

33 —— to the nearest 10 ——→ [ ]

What about the number 35? This is exactly halfway between 30 and 40 but there is a rule that we must follow: If the number is halfway, round UP. So...

... 35 —— to the nearest 10 ——→ **40**

Try these:

85 —— to the nearest 10 ——→ [ ]

45 —— to the nearest 10 ——→ [ ]

25 —— to the nearest 10 ——→ [ ]

375 —— to the nearest 10 ——→ [ ]

425 —— to the nearest 10 ——→ [ ]

Andrew Brodie: Number Journey for ages 7-8 © A&C Black Publishers Ltd 2008

Rounding two-digit or three-digit numbers to the nearest 10 or 100

Worksheet 2

Name: _____

Date: _____

Sometimes we need to round numbers to the nearest 100.
Look at the number line.

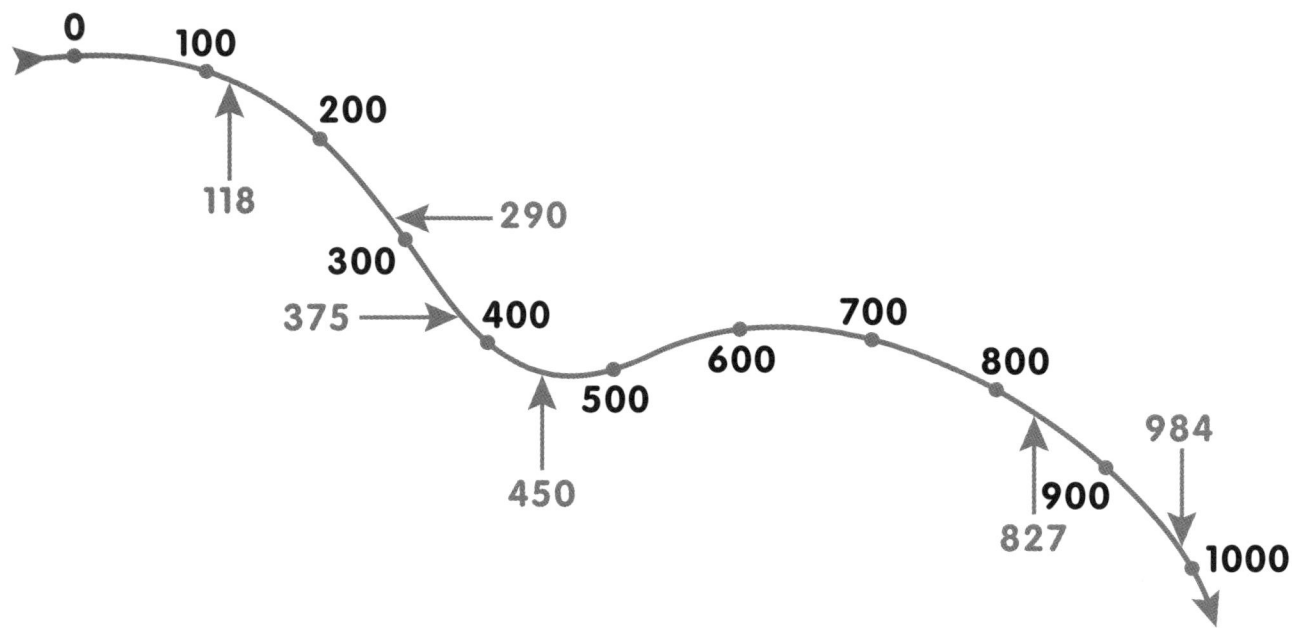

You can see that the number 290 is between 200 and 300. The numbers 200 and 300 are both multiples of 100. The number 290 is closer to 300 so...

... 290 —— to the nearest 100 ——▶ 300

Try these:

375 —— to the nearest 100 ——▶ [ ]

118 —— to the nearest 100 ——▶ [ ]

984 —— to the nearest 100 ——▶ [ ]

What about the number 450? This is exactly halfway between 400 and 500. Do you remember the rule we must follow? If the number is halfway round UP. So...

... 450 —— to the nearest 100 ——▶ [ ]

I can...

I can round two-digit numbers to the nearest 10. ☐
I can round three-digit numbers to the nearest 10. ☐
I can round three-digit numbers to the nearest 100. ☐

Andrew Brodie: Number Journey for ages 7-8 © A&C Black Publishers Ltd 2008

Reading and writing proper fractions

Teacher's notes

Building on previous learning
Before starting this unit check that the children can already:
- use the vocabulary of halves and quarters in context
- find one half, one quarter and three quarters of shapes and sets of objects

Learning objectives
- Read and write proper fractions.
- Interpret the denominator as parts of the whole.
- Interpret the numerator as the number of parts.

Learning outcomes
The children will be able to:
- read proper fractions recognising that the denominator identifies the number of parts into which a whole shape has been divided and that the numerator identifies the number of parts that are specified.
- write proper fractions.

Success criteria
Can the children…

…read fractions such as $\frac{2}{7}, \frac{4}{10}, \frac{1}{4}, \frac{3}{5}, \frac{7}{8}, \frac{1}{3}, \frac{1}{2}, \frac{5}{6}, \frac{5}{9}$?

…write fractions such as $\frac{5}{7}, \frac{6}{10}, \frac{3}{4}, \frac{2}{5}, \frac{1}{8}, \frac{2}{3}, \frac{1}{2}, \frac{1}{6}, \frac{4}{9}$?

Resources needed
- Circles of paper to fold for making halves, quarters, eighths and sixteenths. These provide an excellent method of demonstrating the fact that one half is the same as two quarters, four eighths or eight sixteenths, etc.

Opportunities for using and applying the skills
- Identifying patterns and relationships involving numbers or shapes, and using these to solve problems.

Andrew Brodie: Number Journey for ages 7-8 © A&C Black Publishers Ltd 2008

Reading and writing proper fractions

Help at home sheet

Child's name: **Date:**

Dear Parents

At school we follow the National Curriculum and the Primary Framework for mathematics. One aspect of our work in mathematics is the learning of number skills, including learning to read and write proper fractions. We are keen to involve parents in their children's learning so you may like to help your child by using some of the ideas on this sheet.

National Curriculum

The Primary Framework for mathematics says that Year 3 pupils should:

- read and write proper fractions (e.g. $\frac{3}{7}$, $\frac{9}{10}$) interpreting the denominator as the parts of the whole and the numerator as the number of parts;
- identify and estimate fractions of shapes; use diagrams to compare fractions and establish equivalents.

You could...

… remind your child about halves and quarters when cutting cakes or pizzas.

Explain to your child that the pizza has been cut into four quarters and remind him/her that one quarter can be written like this:

This shows that we have one piece.   ⟶ $\dfrac{1}{4}$ ⟵ This shows that the whole pizza has been cut into four pieces altogether.

… talk to your child about fractions. "If we cut a pizza into quarters how many pieces would there be? If we eat one piece, how much of the pizza would we have left?" Encourage your child to realise that there would be three quarters left and that can be written like this:

This shows that we have three pieces.   ⟶ $\dfrac{3}{4}$ ⟵ This shows that the whole pizza has been cut into four pieces altogether.

… take as many opportunities as possible to talk about fractions when you are preparing food that can be cut into fractional pieces.

You may like to let us know how your child gets on with these activities – if so please return this sheet with any comments on the back.

Andrew Brodie: Number Journey for ages 7-8 © A&C Black Publishers Ltd 2008

Reading and writing proper fractions

Worksheet 1

Name: _____

Date: _____

On this page I will be reading and writing fractions.

Look at this fraction cake:

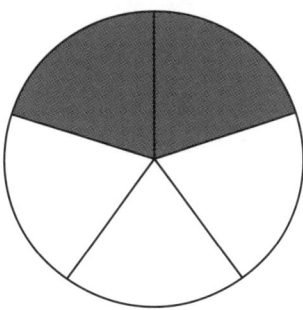

Look at this fraction:

This shows that
two pieces are
shaded. ➤

$$\frac{2}{5}$$

◄ This shows that the
whole fraction cake
has been cut into five
pieces altogether.

What fraction of the cake is not shaded?

This shows that
three pieces are
not shaded. ➤

$$\frac{3}{5}$$

◄ This shows that the
whole fraction cake
has been cut into five
pieces altogether.

Look at the fraction cakes below and write the correct fractions.

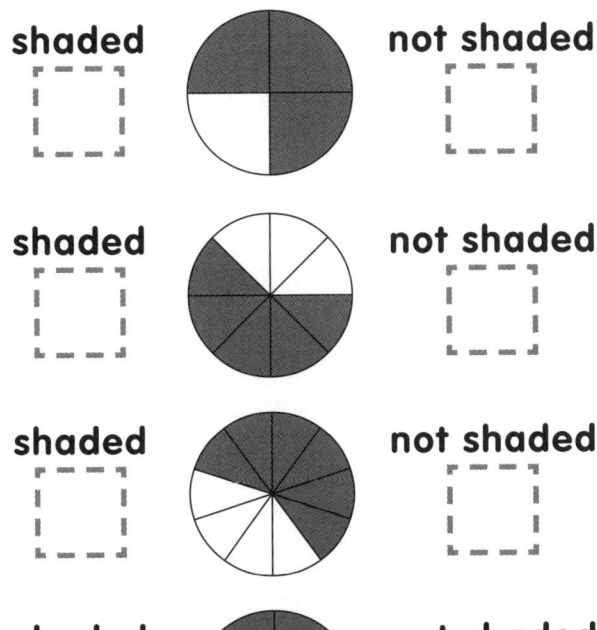
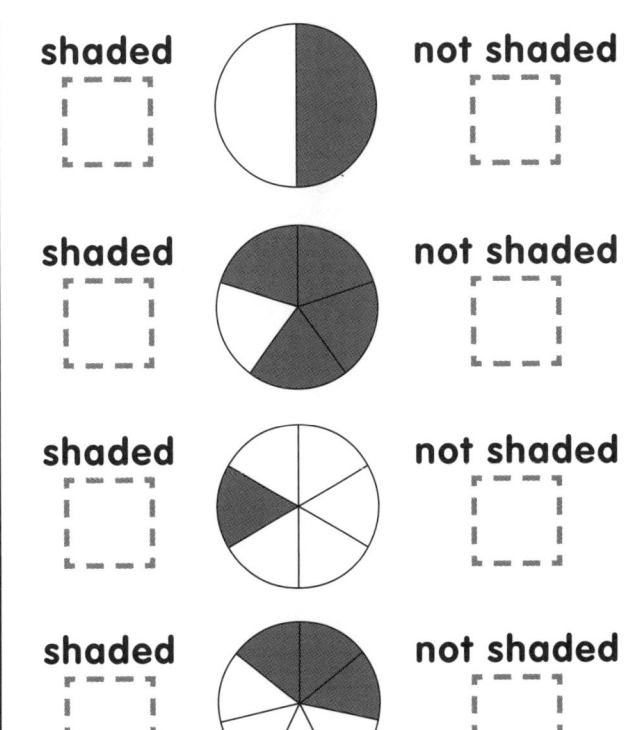

shaded ☐   not shaded ☐   shaded ☐   not shaded ☐

shaded ☐   not shaded ☐   shaded ☐   not shaded ☐

shaded ☐   not shaded ☐   shaded ☐   not shaded ☐

shaded ☐   not shaded ☐   shaded ☐   not shaded ☐

Andrew Brodie: Number Journey for ages 7-8 © A&C Black Publishers Ltd 2008

Reading and writing proper fractions

Name: _____

Date: _____

Shade each of the fraction cakes by the fraction shown.
Write what fraction of each cake is not shaded.

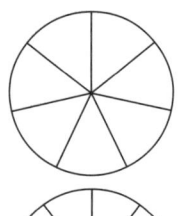 $\dfrac{2}{7}$ is shaded [ ] not shaded

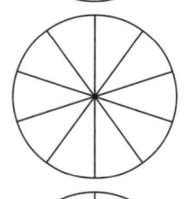 $\dfrac{4}{10}$ is shaded [ ] not shaded

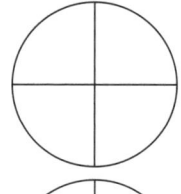 $\dfrac{1}{4}$ is shaded [ ] not shaded

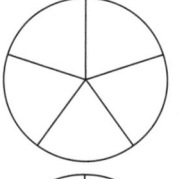 $\dfrac{3}{5}$ is shaded [ ] not shaded

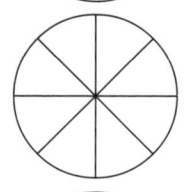 $\dfrac{7}{8}$ is shaded [ ] not shaded

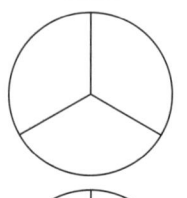 $\dfrac{1}{3}$ is shaded [ ] not shaded

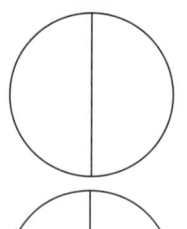 $\dfrac{1}{2}$ is shaded [ ] not shaded

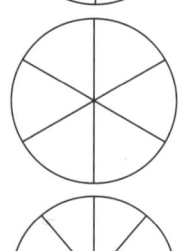 $\dfrac{5}{6}$ is shaded [ ] not shaded

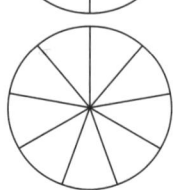 $\dfrac{5}{9}$ is shaded [ ] not shaded

I can... I can read fractions. ☐
I can write fractions. ☐

Addition facts for numbers to 20

Teacher's notes

Building on previous learning

Before starting this unit check that the children can already:
- derive and recall all pairs of numbers with totals to 20
- derive and recall all addition and subtraction facts for each number to at least 10

Learning objectives

- Derive and recall all addition facts for each number to 20.
- Calculate the value of an unknown in a number sentence.

Learning outcomes

- The children will be able to recall all pairs of numbers that add together to make 20.
- Using this knowledge and their knowledge of addition facts to 10 they will be able to find all pairs of numbers that add together to make numbers 11 to 19.

Success criteria

Can the children…
…recall the addition pairs for 20?
…find the addition pairs for 13, 15 and 18?
…recall the addition pairs for numbers up to 20? (Note that 'recall' does not necessarily mean to remember without thinking – what we are seeking is for the child to have a strategy for retrieving the number facts quickly and efficiently.)

Resources needed

- Counters, marbles, etc for counting.
- A class number line.
- Individual number lines. It's a good idea to have a number line from 0 to 20 stuck to each child's table with sticky-backed plastic.

Opportunities for using and applying the skills

- Presenting solutions to puzzles and problems in an organised way.
- Explaining decisions, methods and results in pictorial, spoken or written form, using mathematical language and number sentences.
- Describing patterns and relationships involving numbers.

Andrew Brodie: Number Journey for ages 7-8 © A&C Black Publishers Ltd 2008

Addition facts for numbers to 20

Help at home sheet

Child's name: Date:

Dear Parents
At school we follow the National Curriculum and the Primary Framework for mathematics. One aspect of our work in mathematics is the learning of number skills, including practising addition facts up to 20. We are keen to involve parents in their children's learning so you may like to help your child by using some of the ideas on this sheet.

National Curriculum

The Primary Framework for mathematics says that Year 3 pupils should:
• derive and recall all addition facts for each number to 20.

You could...

...make a number line with your child showing all numbers from 0 to 20.

...practise the following questions with your child. Allow your child to use their fingers if necessary or to count on or back using the number line that you've made. Do one column of questions then check them through with your child, giving advice on how to answer them e.g. he/she should start with the lower of the two numbers then count on to the bigger number or start with the bigger number and count back to the smaller number. Praise your child for any success before tackling the next column. If you find that he/she is very confident, you could try timing to see how quickly he/she can complete each column.

$15 + 4 =$	$5 + 5 =$	$11 + 4 =$	$9 + 4 =$
$16 + 2 =$	$8 + 4 =$	$9 + 2 =$	$18 + 2 =$
$7 + 5 =$	$16 + 4 =$	$7 + 7 =$	$15 + 5 =$
$14 + 1 =$	$12 + 3 =$	$13 + 4 =$	$13 + 3 =$
$9 + 7 =$	$10 + 6 =$	$9 + 9 =$	$9 + 5 =$
$13 + 6 =$	$7 + 6 =$	$16 + 2 =$	$8 + 8 =$
$8 + 4 =$	$9 + 4 =$	$8 + 7 =$	$14 + 4 =$
$6 + 6 =$	$8 + 6 =$	$9 + 6 =$	$6 + 9 =$

You may like to let us know how your child gets on with these activities – if so please return this sheet with any comments on the back.

Andrew Brodie: Number Journey for ages 7-8 © A&C Black Publishers Ltd 2008

Addition facts for numbers to 20

Worksheet 1

Name: _____

Date: _____

On this page I will be finding pairs of numbers that make 15.
On this page I will be finding pairs of numbers that make 18.

Write all the addition facts that use pairs of numbers to make 15.
Two facts have been written for you.

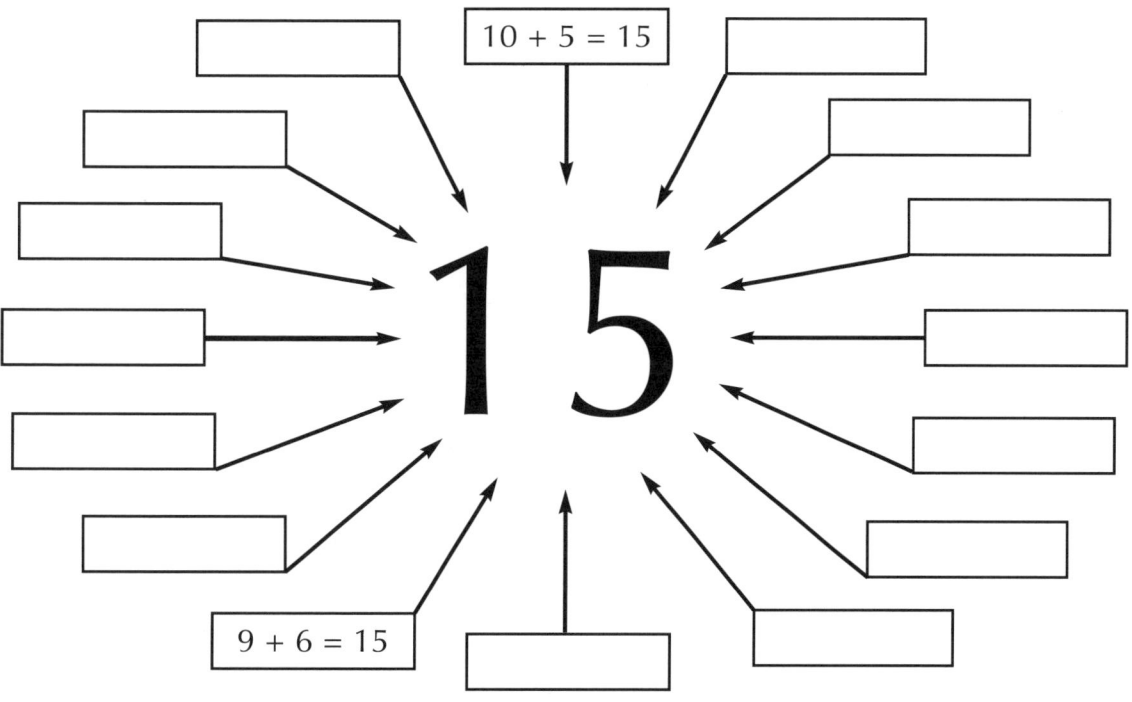

10 + 5 = 15

9 + 6 = 15

Write all the addition facts that use pairs of numbers to make 18.
Two facts have been written for you.

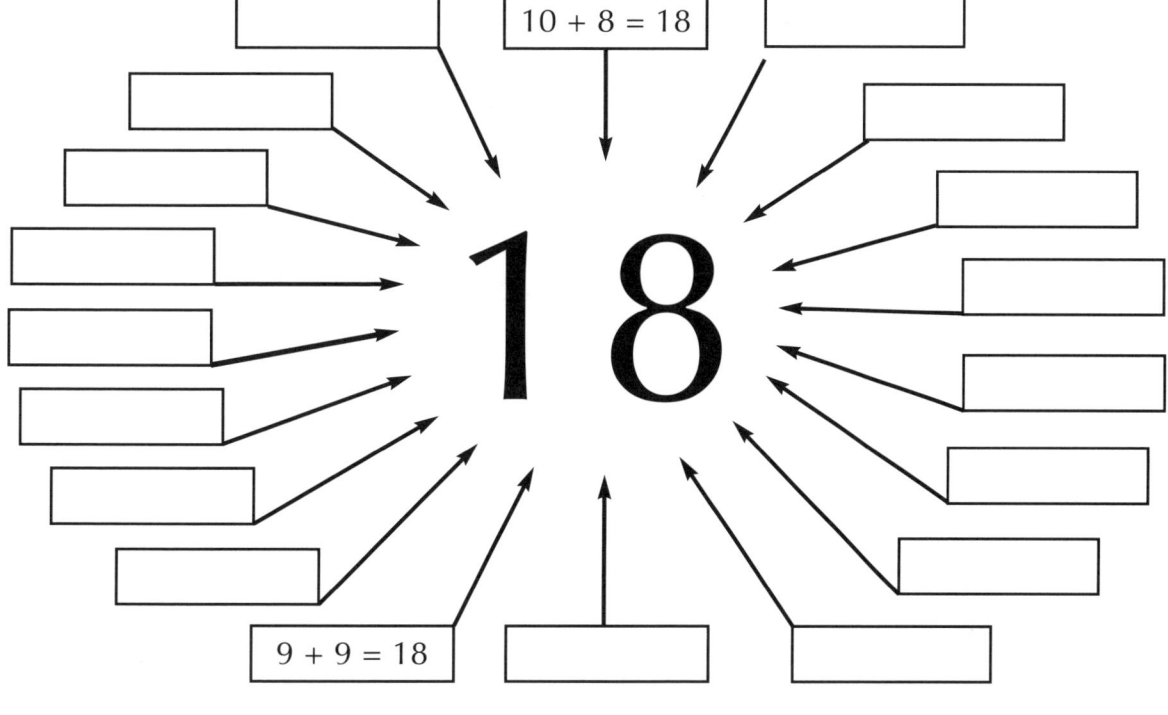

10 + 8 = 18

9 + 9 = 18

Andrew Brodie: Number Journey for ages 7-8 © A&C Black Publishers Ltd 2008

Addition facts for numbers to 20

Name: _____

Date: _____

Find the addition pairs for number 13. Two facts have been written for you.

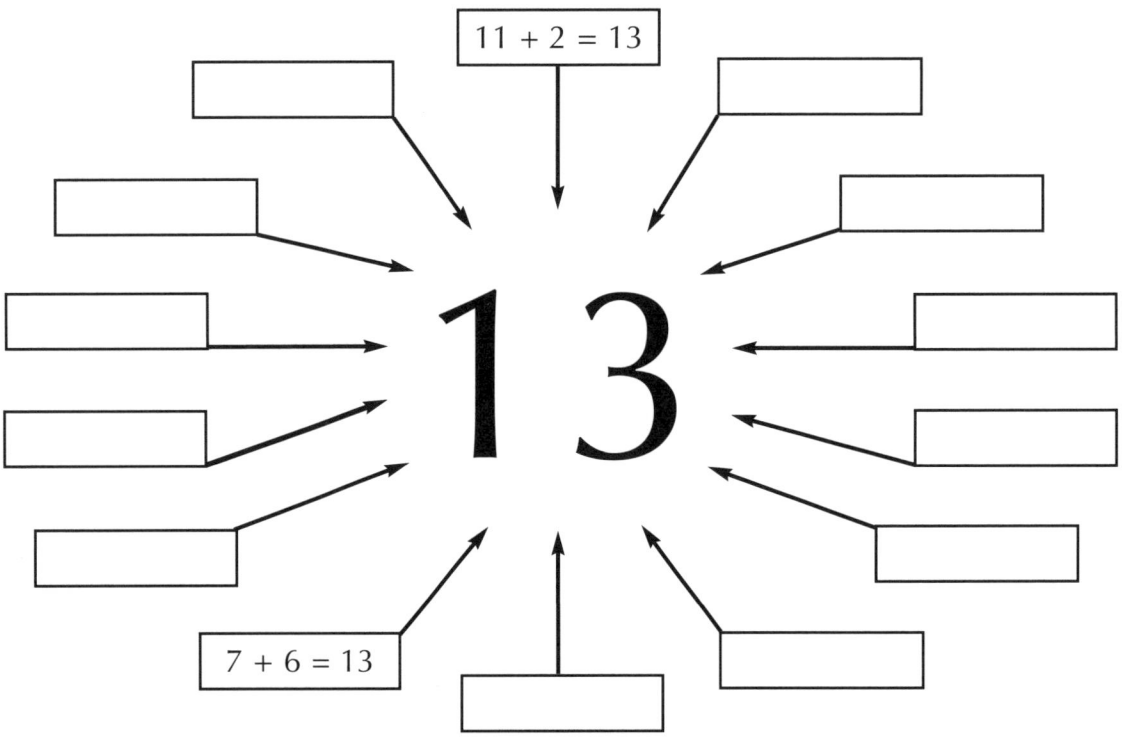

11 + 2 = 13

13

7 + 6 = 13

Answer these questions by writing the correct numbers in the boxes.

16 + [ ] = 20   17 + [ ] = 20   15 + [ ] = 20

14 + [ ] = 20   7 + [ ] = 13   5 + [ ] = 12

17 + [ ] = 19   6 + [ ] = 14   12 + [ ] = 15

15 + [ ] = 19   8 + [ ] = 16   9 + [ ] = 14

I can...   I can recall addition pairs for 20.   [ ]
I can find addition pairs for numbers up to 20.   [ ]

Andrew Brodie: Number Journey for ages 7-8 © A&C Black Publishers Ltd 2008

Subtraction facts for numbers to 20

Teacher's notes

Building on previous learning
Before starting this unit check that the children can already:
- derive and recall all pairs of numbers with totals to 20
- derive and recall all addition and subtraction facts for each number to at least 10

Learning objectives
- Derive and recall all subtraction facts for numbers up to 20.
- Calculate the value of an unknown in a number sentence.

Learning outcomes
- The children will be able to find all subtraction facts from 20.
- Using this knowledge and their knowledge of subtraction facts to 10 they will be able to find all subtraction facts for the numbers 11 to 19.

Success criteria
Can the children…
…recall the subtractions from 20?
…find the subtractions from 11, 16 and 19?
…recall the subtractions for numbers up to 20? (Note that 'recall' does not necessarily mean to remember without thinking – what we are seeking is for the child to have a strategy for retrieving the number facts quickly and efficiently.)

Resources needed
- Counters, marbles, etc for counting.
- A class number line.
- Individual number lines. It's a good idea is to have a number line from 0 to 20 stuck to each child's table with sticky-backed plastic.

Opportunities for using and applying the skills
- Presenting solutions to puzzles and problems in an organised way.
- Explaining decisions, methods and results in pictorial, spoken or written form, using mathematical language and number sentences.
- Describing patterns and relationships involving numbers.
- Solving problems involving subtraction in the context of money e.g. finding change from 20p.

Andrew Brodie: Number Journey for ages 7-8 © A&C Black Publishers Ltd 2008

Subtraction facts for numbers to 20

Help at home sheet

Child's name: Date:

Dear Parents
At school we follow the National Curriculum and the Primary Framework for mathematics. One aspect of our work in mathematics is the learning of number skills, including practising subtraction facts up to 20. We are keen to involve parents in their children's learning so you may like to help your child by using some of the ideas on this sheet.

National Curriculum

The Primary Framework for mathematics says that Year 3 pupils should:
• derive and recall all subtraction facts for each number to 20.

You could...

… give your child some practice in finding change from 20p.

… make a number line with your child showing all numbers from 0 to 20.

… practise the following questions with your child. Allow your child to use their fingers if necessary or to count on or back using the number line that you've made. Do one column of questions then check them through with your child, giving advice on how to answer them e.g. he/she should start with the lower of the two numbers then count on to the bigger number or start with the bigger number and count back to the smaller number. Praise your child for any success before tackling the next column. If you find that he/she is very confident, you could try timing to see how quickly he/she can complete each column.

20 − 7 =	18 − 9 =	19 − 9 =	12 − 3 =
13 − 5 =	16 − 4 =	17 − 8 =	20 − 8 =
10 − 7 =	13 − 7 =	11 − 6 =	16 − 9 =
16 − 8 =	20 − 9 =	14 − 5 =	13 − 8 =
12 − 9 =	12 − 5 =	15 − 8 =	10 − 8 =
14 − 8 =	14 − 8 =	12 − 9 =	14 − 5 =
17 − 9 =	10 − 6 =	10 − 4 =	18 − 10 =
15 − 6 =	11 − 5 =	16 − 7 =	15 − 9 =

You may like to let us know how your child gets on with these activities – if so please return this sheet with any comments on the back.

Andrew Brodie: Number Journey for ages 7-8 © A&C Black Publishers Ltd 2008

Subtraction facts for numbers to 20

Worksheet 1

Name: _____

Date: _____

On this page I will be finding subtractions from 11.
On this page I will be finding subtractions from 16.

Write all the subtraction from 11 facts. Two facts have been written for you.

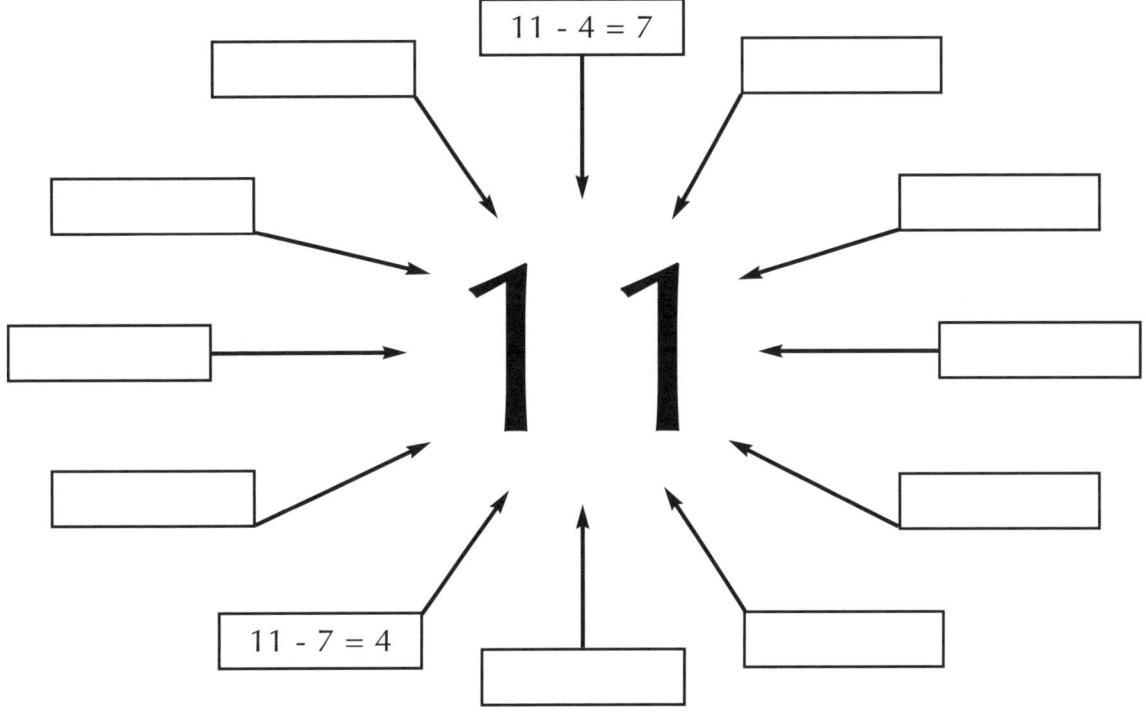

11 - 4 = 7

11 - 7 = 4

Write all the subtraction from 16 facts. Two facts have been written for you.

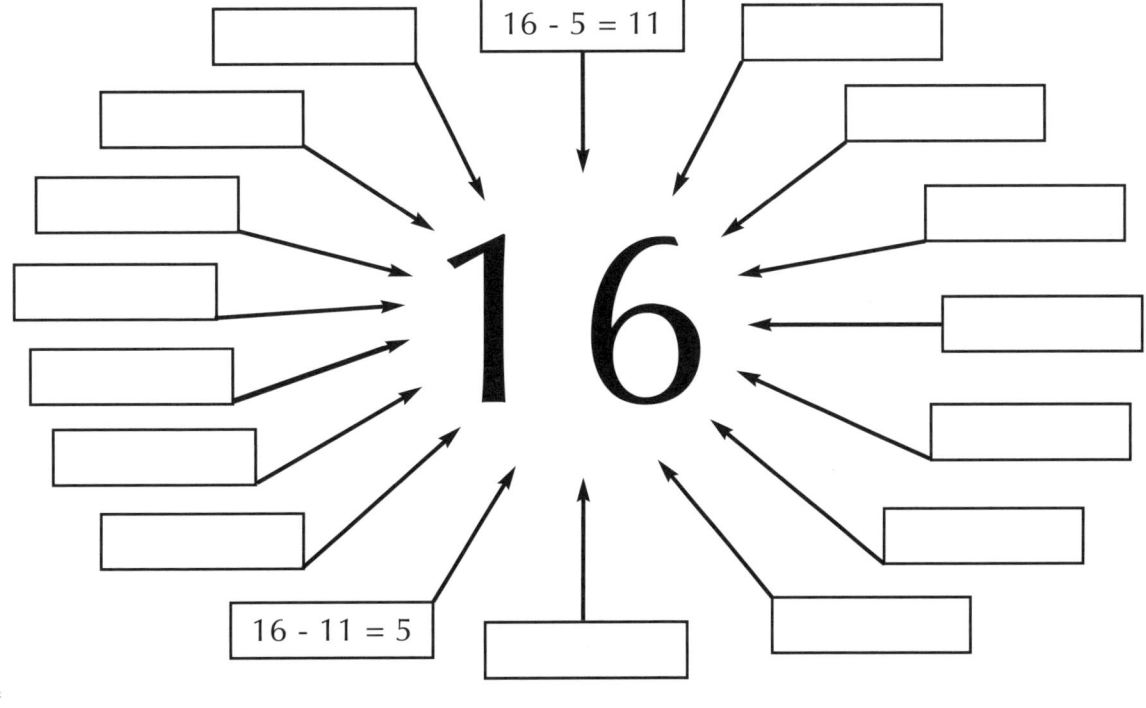

16 - 5 = 11

16 - 11 = 5

Andrew Brodie: Number Journey for ages 7-8 © A&C Black Publishers Ltd 2008

Subtraction facts for numbers to 20

Name: _____

Date: _____

Find the subtraction from 19 facts. Two facts have been written for you.

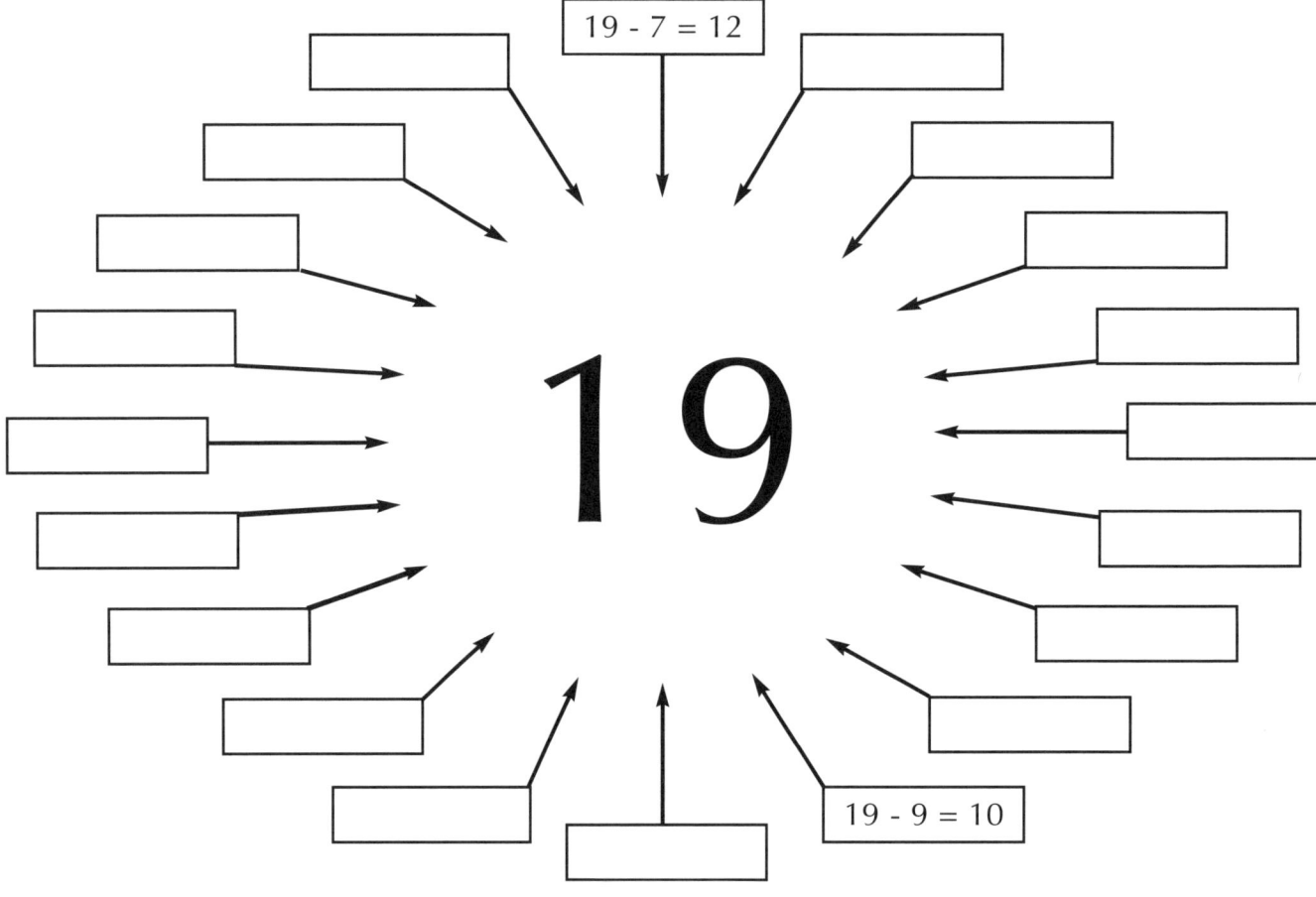

$19 - 7 = 12$

$19 - 9 = 10$

Answer these questions by writing the correct numbers in the boxes.

20 - 19 = ☐   20 - 6 = ☐   20 - 9 = ☐

20 - 10 = ☐   12 - 6 = ☐   14 - 8 = ☐

19 - 6 = ☐   16 - 9 = ☐   13 - 4 = ☐

11 - 8 = ☐   20 - 11 = ☐   17 - 14 = ☐

 I can...

I can recall subtractions from 20. ☐
I can find subtractions from numbers up to 20. ☐

Addition and subtraction facts for pairs of multiples of 10

Teacher's notes

Building on previous learning
Before starting this unit check that the children can already:
- derive and recall all pairs of multiples of 10 with totals up to 100
- recognise multiples of 10

Learning objectives
- Derive and recall sums and differences of multiples of 10.
- Calculate the value of an unknown in a number sentence.

Learning outcomes
The children will be able to:
- add together multiples of 10 up to at least 200.
- find the difference between multiples of 10 where the larger number is up to at least 200.

Success criteria
Can the children…
…complete the following additions of multiples of 10: 90 + 90, 90 + 40, 90 + 80, 90 + 60, 90 + 50, 90 + 20?
…find the differences between the following pairs of multiples of 10: 120, 90   160, 70   220, 180   130, 60   120, 50   140, 60   210, 170   420, 390   510, 470   880, 790   250, 120   310, 200?

Resources needed
- 10p, 20p and 50p coins.
- A class number line up to 1000 – you may like to discuss the questions on the worksheets making reference to this number line before the children start. Take the opportunity to raise pupils' awareness of the fact that subtraction is the inverse of addition e.g. when they add 90 and 40 to make 130, ask them to subtract 40 from 130 to find 90 or to subtract 90 from 130 to find 40.

Opportunities for using and applying the skills
- Solving one-step and two-step problems involving numbers, money or measures.
- Identifying patterns and relationships involving numbers e.g. noticing that 7 + 8 = 15 is similar to 70 + 80 = 150.

33

Addition and subtraction facts for pairs of multiples of 10

Help at home sheet

Child's name: **Date:**

Dear Parents

At school we follow the National Curriculum and the Primary Framework for mathematics. One aspect of our work in mathematics is the learning of number skills, including finding the sums and differences of multiples of 10 e.g. 80 + 50 = 130 and 130 − 50 = 80. We are keen to involve parents in their children's learning so you may like to help your child by using some of the ideas on this sheet.

National Curriculum

The Primary Framework for mathematics says that Year 3 pupils should:
• derive and recall sums and differences of multiples of 10.

You could...

… use 10p, 20p and 50p coins to help your child to calculate quickly in multiples of 10. At this stage it is best to work only in pence, rather than in pounds and pence.

Ask your child questions such as:

'What's 50 pence plus 20 pence?'
'What's 50 pence minus 20 pence?'
'If I have four 20 pence coins, how much have I got altogether?'
'If I spend 30 pence, how much would I have left?'

If you feel that your child is confident, you could begin to ask questions involving pounds and pence:

'I've got 90 pence and 70 pence. How much have I got altogether?'
'I've got three 50 pence coins. How much have I got altogether?'
'How much more is one pound than 20 pence?'

You may like to let us know how your child gets on with these activities – if so please return this sheet with any comments on the back.

Andrew Brodie: Number Journey for ages 7-8 © A&C Black Publishers Ltd 2008

Addition and subtraction facts for pairs of multiples of 10

Worksheet 1

Name: _____

Date: _____

On this page I will be adding together multiples of 10.

Complete these addition sparklers. One of the answers is provided for you.

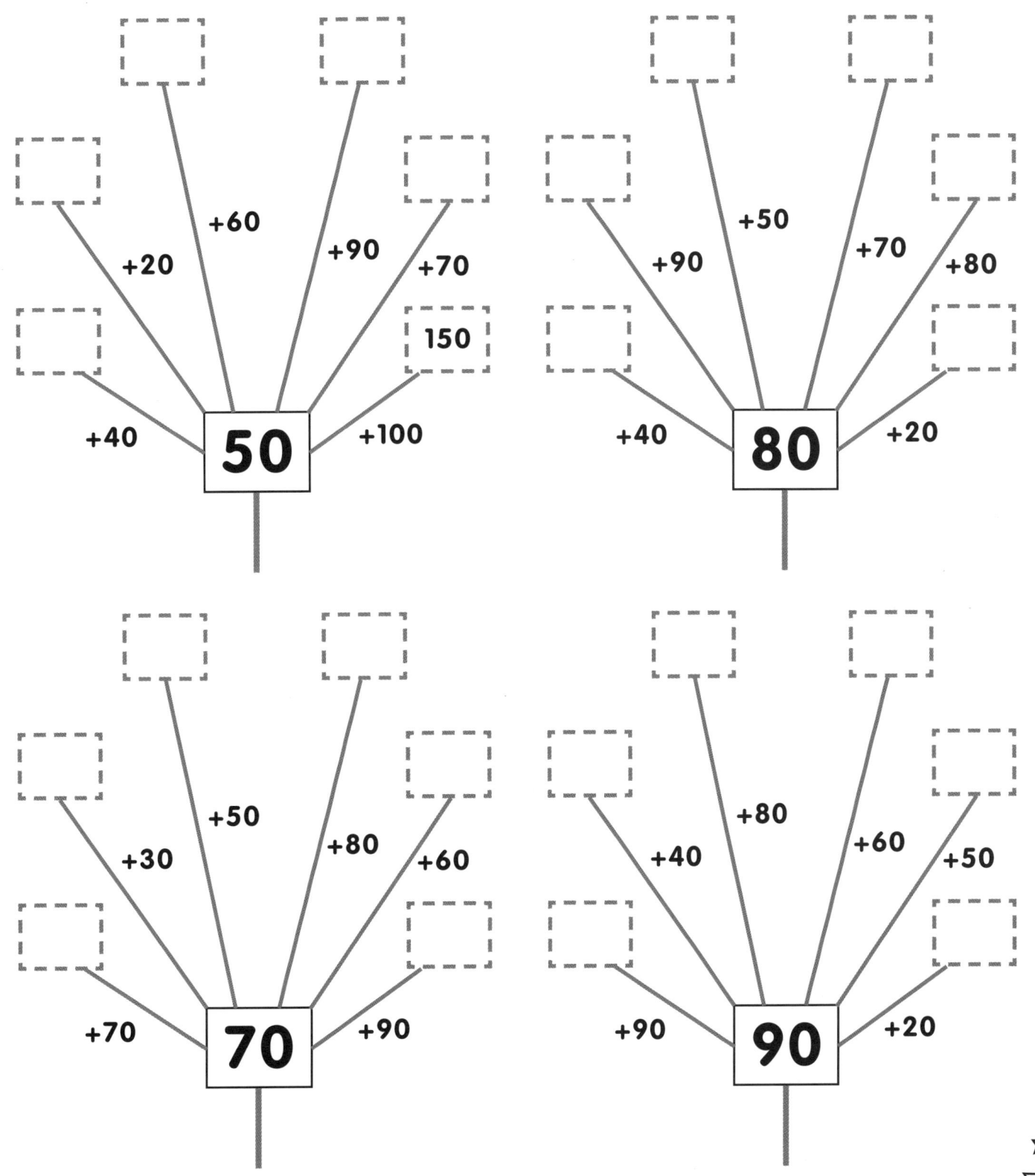

Andrew Brodie: Number Journey for ages 7-8 © A&C Black Publishers Ltd 2008

Addition and subtraction facts for pairs of multiples of 10

Worksheet 2

Name: _____

Date: _____

Find the differences. The first one has been done for you.

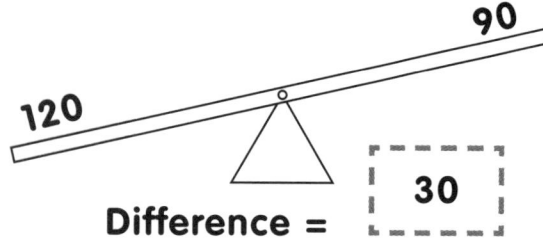

90

120

Difference = 30

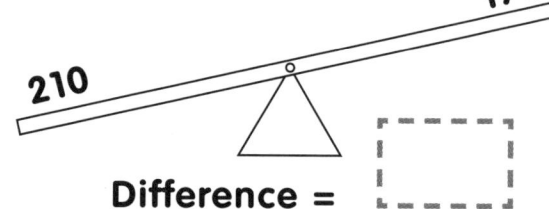

170

210

Difference =

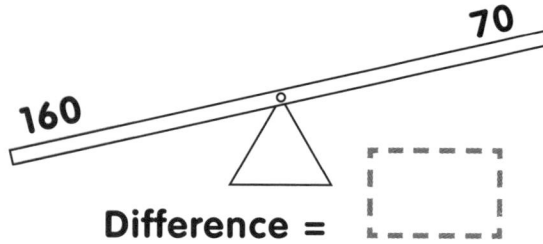

70

160

Difference =

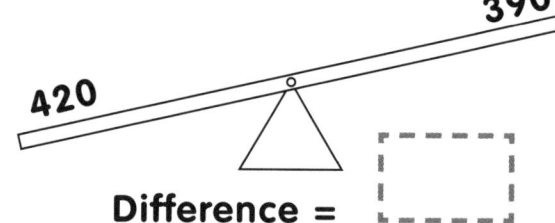

390

420

Difference =

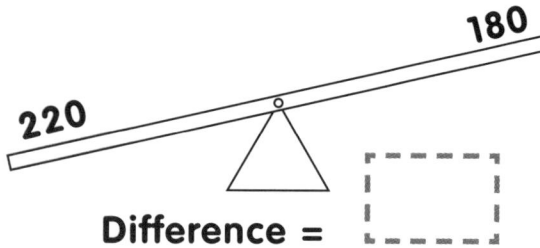

180

220

Difference =

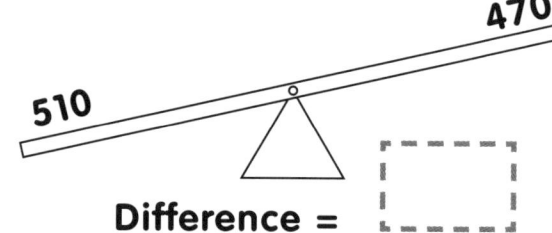

470

510

Difference =

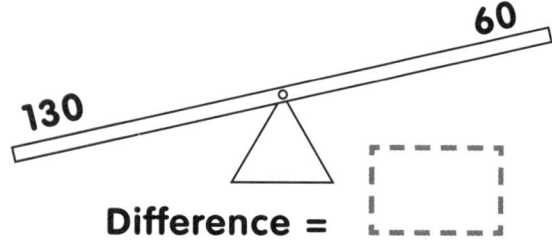

60

130

Difference =

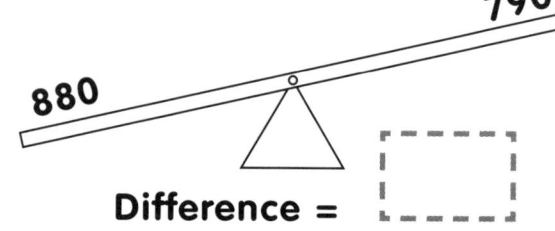

790

880

Difference =

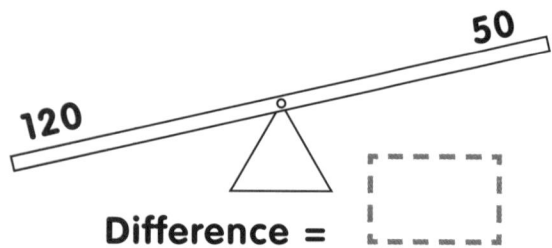

50

120

Difference =

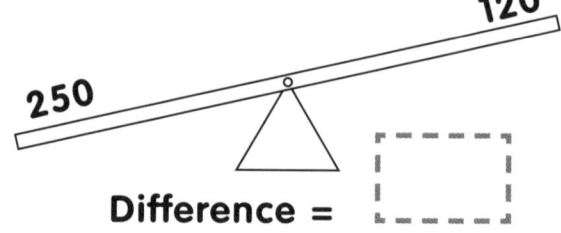

120

250

Difference =

I can...

I can add multiples of 10 together. ☐

I can find the difference between two multiples of 10. ☐

36

Deriving and recalling number pairs that total 100

Teacher's notes

Building on previous learning
Before starting this unit check that the children can already:
- derive and recall all addition and subtraction facts for each number to 20
- derive and recall addition and subtraction facts for all pairs of multiples of 10 with totals to 100
- order two-digit numbers and position them on a number line
- calculate the value of an unknown in a number sentence

Learning objectives
- Derive and recall all addition and subtraction facts for number pairs that total 100.

Learning outcomes
The children will be able to:
- find all pairs of numbers that total 100.
- subtract any one-digit or two-digit number from 100.

Success criteria
Can the children…

…find number pairs that total 100 e.g. the corresponding number for each of the following numbers: 63, 81, 34, 77, 11, 98, 46, 29, 52?

…find the following subtractions from 100: 100 – 63, 100 – 89, 100 – 42, 100 – 37, 100 – 16, 100 – 51, 100 – 75, 100 – 94, 100 – 28?

Resources needed
- Coins
- Metre rules
- A very clear number line to 100, to be marked with every number if possible. This can be used to help the children when they first approach questions such as 63 + ⬚ = 100. Realising that subtraction is the inverse of addition, many older children will produce the incorrect answer 47 as they have gone through the process of subtracting 60 from 100 to find 40, then 3 from 10 to find 7, then combined their results. Here they have made good use of their mental arithmetic knowledge that 100 – 60 = 40 and that 10 – 3 = 7 but they have not followed the logic of the number system. Discussion and use of the number line at Year 3 can often overcome this problem. The children can observe the 'jumps' that must be made to count on from 63 to 70 in seven units then from 70 to 100 in three tens or to count back to 70 from 100 in three tens then back to 63 in seven units.

Opportunities for using and applying the skills
- Solving one-step and two-step problems involving number, money or measures, choosing and carrying out appropriate calculations.

Andrew Brodie: Number Journey for ages 7-8 © A&C Black Publishers Ltd 2008

Deriving and recalling number pairs that total 100

Help at home sheet

Child's name: **Date:**

Dear Parents

At school we follow the National Curriculum and the Primary Framework for mathematics. One aspect of our work in mathematics is the learning of number skills, including finding pairs of numbers that total 100. This is very important in relation to money and finding change and also for measuring in centimetres and metres. We are keen to involve parents in their children's learning so you may like to help your child by using some of the ideas on this sheet.

National Curriculum

The Primary Framework for mathematics says that Year 3 pupils should:
- derive and recall all addition and subtraction facts for each number to 20, sums and differences of multiples of 10 and number pairs that total 100.

You could...

… make a number line with your child showing all numbers from 0 to 100. Pick any multiple of 10 on the number line e.g. 60. Ask your child: 'How many more is 100 than 60?' Help him/her to find out by counting on from 60 to 100, encouraging him/her to make 'jumps' of 10 at a time: '10, 20, 30, 40.' '100 is 40 more than 60.' Now try a harder question by picking a number such as 64. Say: 'That's closer to 100 than 60. How much more is 100 than 64?' Encourage your child to count on 6 units from 64 to reach 70. Say: '70 is 6 more than 64, now let's go on to 100.' Again, your child can now make jumps of 10 at a time: '10, 20, 30.' 'Altogether we have counted on 6 and 30 – that's 36 altogether. So 100 is 36 more than 64.' Keep practising and giving lots of encouragement.

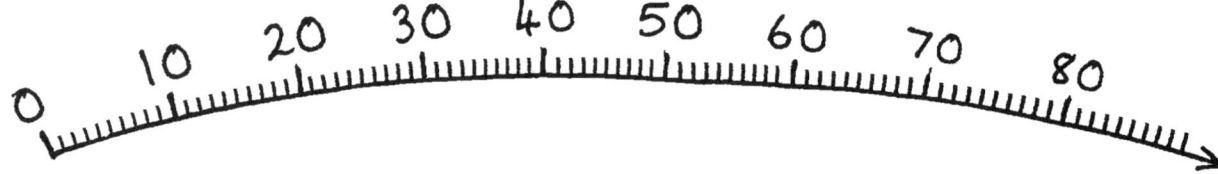

… give your child some practice in finding change from £1: 'If I have £1 and I spend 32p, how much have I got left?' You can help your child by counting back 32, in jumps, from 100 on the number line, or by counting on, in jumps from 32 to 100.

You may like to let us know how your child gets on with these activities – if so please return this sheet with any comments on the back.

Andrew Brodie: Number Journey for ages 7-8 © A&C Black Publishers Ltd 2008

Deriving and recalling number pairs that total 100

Worksheet 1

Name: _____

Date: _____

On this page I will be finding numbers that add together to make 100.

Write the missing numbers in the boxes.

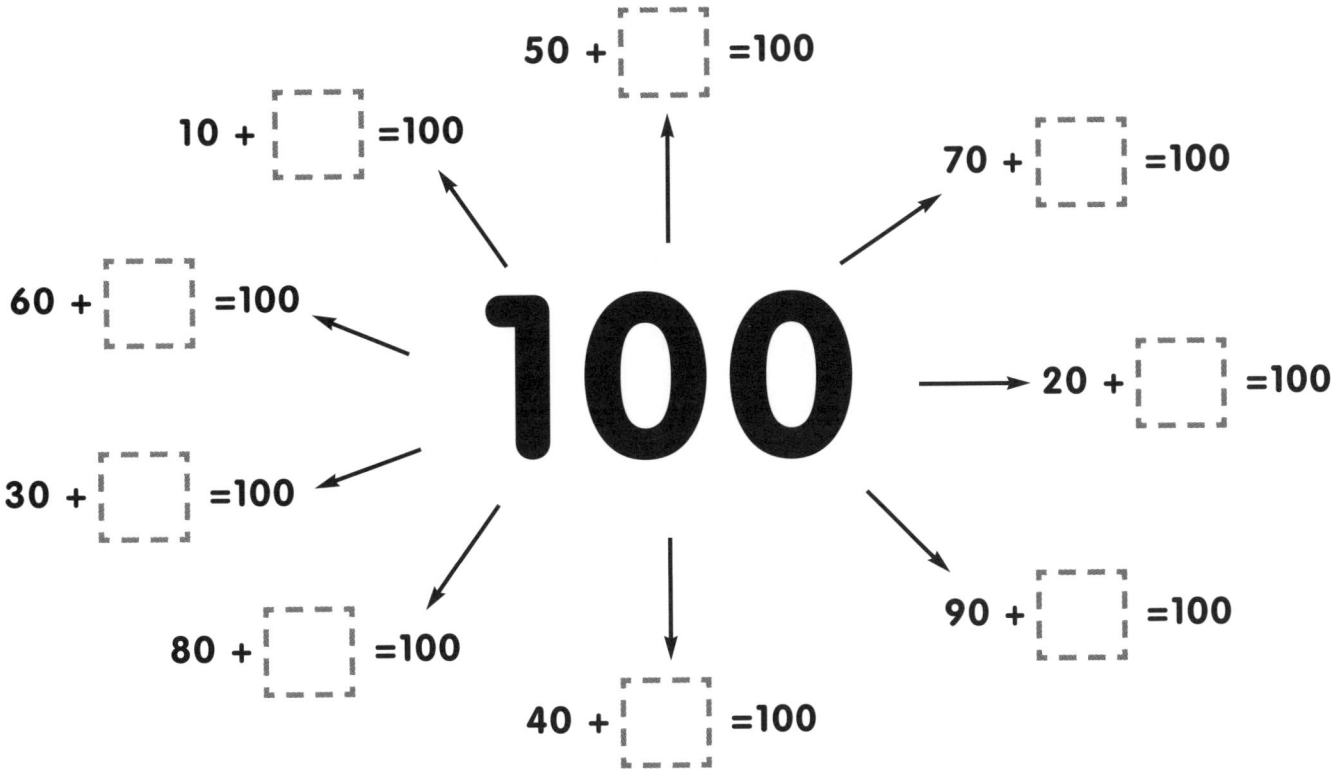

50 + ☐ =100

10 + ☐ =100

70 + ☐ =100

60 + ☐ =100

20 + ☐ =100

30 + ☐ =100

100

80 + ☐ =100

90 + ☐ =100

40 + ☐ =100

Now try these.

63 + ☐ =100

52 + ☐ =100

81 + ☐ =100

29 + ☐ =100

34 + ☐ =100

100

46 + ☐ =100

77 + ☐ =100

98 + ☐ =100

11 + ☐ =100

Andrew Brodie: Number Journey for ages 7-8 © A&C Black Publishers Ltd 2008

Deriving and recalling number pairs that total 100

Worksheet 2

Name: _____

Date: _____

Find the subtractions from 100.

100 - 20 = ☐

100 - 50 = ☐

100 - 10 = ☐

100 - 70 = ☐

100 - 80 = ☐

100 - 30 = ☐

100 - 40 = ☐

100 - 60 = ☐

100 - 100 = ☐

100 - 90 = ☐

Now try these.

100 - 63 = ☐

100 - 89 = ☐

100 - 28 = ☐

100 - 42 = ☐

100 - 94 = ☐

100 - 37 = ☐

100 - 75 = ☐

100 - 51 = ☐

100 - 16 = ☐

 I can...

I can subtract multiples of 10 from 100. ☐

I can subtract any two-digit number from 100. ☐

Andrew Brodie: Number Journey for ages 7-8 © A&C Black Publishers Ltd 2008

Adding and subtracting mentally one-digit and two-digit numbers

Teacher's notes

Building on previous learning
Before starting this unit check that the children can already:
- add or subtract mentally a one-digit number or a multiple of 10 to or from any two-digit number
- recall all addition and subtraction facts for each number to at least 10

Learning objectives
- Add mentally combinations of one-digit and two-digit numbers.
- Subtract mentally combinations of one-digit and two-digit numbers.

Learning outcomes
The children will be able to:
- use a variety of techniques for adding a string of one-digit and/or two-digit numbers together.
- use their knowledge of addition and subtraction facts to subtract any one-digit or two-digit number from a larger two-digit number.

Success criteria
Can the children…

…use successful techniques to add mentally combinations of one-digit and two-digit numbers in questions such as 12 + 6 + 8 + 3 + 4?

…subtract 9 from 50, 71, 52, 63, 64, 95, 46, 87, 78, 99?

…subtract 11 from 40, 81, 52, 32, 53, 44, 15, 36, 27, 68, 89?

Resources needed
- A class number line from 0 to at least 100. Encourage the children to realise that addition can be done in any order e.g. if required to add together 23, 4 and 8: you could add the 23 to the 4 then add the 8; you could add the 4 and 8 together then add the answer to 23; you could add 23 to 8 then add the 4.

  Help the children to find appropriate techniques for adding a string of numbers such as 12 + 6 + 8 + 3 + 4. Here, some children quickly respond to the idea of finding the multiples of 10: 12 + 8 = 20 and 6 + 4 = 10 which makes a total of 30, then add the 3 to make a final answer of 33. However, others find it easier and just as effective to 'work along the row': 12 + 6 = 18, then 18 + 8 = 26, then 26 + 3 = 29, then 29 + 4 = 33. For children who are confident with number facts either method is perfectly acceptable. With the subtractions, we have focussed on subtracting 9 or subtracting 11. With subtracting 9 you may wish to show the children that they can subtract 10 but then 'give one back' because only 9 should have been subtracted. With subtracting 11 they can subtract 10 then another 1. If you use a number line to demonstrate they will see the logic of both processes.

Opportunities for using and applying the skills
- Solving one-step and two-step problems involving numbers, money or measures.
- choosing and carrying out appropriate calculations.
- Identifying patterns and relationships involving numbers and using these to solve problems.
- The final question on Worksheet 1 can be used as an extension activity for more able pupils. Can they see the pattern in the questions? Can they see the pattern in the answers? The answers form the sequence of triangular numbers.

Andrew Brodie: Number Journey for ages 7-8 © A&C Black Publishers Ltd 2008

Adding and subtracting mentally one-digit and two-digit numbers

Help at home sheet

Child's name: **Date:**

Dear Parents

At school we follow the National Curriculum and the Primary Framework for mathematics. One aspect of our work in mathematics is the learning of number skills, including practising adding or subtracting mentally one-digit and two-digit numbers. We are keen to involve parents in their children's learning so you may like to help your child by using some of the ideas on this sheet.

National Curriculum

The Primary Framework for mathematics says that Year 3 pupils should:
- add or subtract mentally combinations of one-digit and two-digit numbers.

You could...

… practise the following questions with your child. Allow your child to use their fingers if they need to. Do one column of questions then go through them with your child, giving advice on how to answer them. Encourage him/her to look carefully at each question to see if it has an addition or subtraction sign. Praise your child for any success. If you find that he/she is very confident, you could try setting a timer to see how quickly he/she can complete each column of questions.

$26 + 5 =$	$63 - 7 =$	$91 - 5 =$	$47 + 6 + 3 =$
$39 + 7 =$	$70 - 11 =$	$47 + 6 + 6 =$	$53 - 8 =$
$12 + 9 + 4 =$	$19 + 5 + 11 =$	$81 - 11 =$	$29 + 9 + 9 =$
$31 - 5 =$	$72 - 8 =$	$62 - 9 =$	$8 + 8 + 8 =$
$42 - 8 =$	$48 + 9 =$	$17 + 5 + 3 =$	$23 - 8 =$
$16 + 3 + 4 =$	$18 + 5 + 2 =$	$26 + 8 + 2 =$	$35 + 6 + 5 =$
$52 - 9 =$	$74 + 9 + 6 =$	$41 - 9 =$	$54 - 9 =$
$31 - 6 + 9 =$	$62 + 9 + 3 =$	$82 - 9 =$	$27 + 13 =$

You may like to let us know how your child gets on with these activities – if so please return this sheet with any comments on the back.

Andrew Brodie: Number Journey for ages 7-8 © A&C Black Publishers Ltd 2008

Adding and subtracting mentally one-digit and two-digit numbers

Worksheet 1

Name: _____

Date: _____

On this page I will be adding strings of numbers together.

Look at this addition question: $4 + 5 + 6 + 7 =$

You could do $4 + 5$ then $+ 6$ then $+ 7$.

Try it: $4 + 5 + 6 + 7 =$ ☐

or

You could add the 4 and 6 together then $+ 5$ then $+ 7$.

Try it: $4 + 5 + 6 + 7 =$ ☐

Now try these questions. Remember, you can choose which order to add the numbers.

$14 + 9 + 6 + 3 =$ ☐ $25 + 7 + 8 =$ ☐

$3 + 9 + 17 + 4 =$ ☐ $8 + 7 + 5 + 23 =$ ☐

$6 + 35 + 1 + 7 + 4 =$ ☐ $9 + 5 + 32 =$ ☐

$82 + 5 + 6 =$ ☐ $19 + 3 + 11 + 4 =$ ☐

Look at the questions below very carefully. Can you find a quick way to answer them?

$10 + 10 + 10 + 10 =$ ☐ $11 + 11 + 11 + 11 =$ ☐

$12 + 12 + 12 + 12 =$ ☐ $13 + 13 + 13 + 13 =$ ☐

Look at the pattern made by the questions below. Can you continue the pattern?

$$1$$
$$1 + 2 = 3$$
$$1 + 2 + 3 = 6$$
$$1 + 2 + 3 + 4 =$$

Andrew Brodie: Number Journey for ages 7-8 © A&C Black Publishers Ltd 2008

Adding and subtracting mentally one-digit and two-digit numbers

Worksheet 2

Name: _____

Date: _____

1	2	3	4	5	6	7	8	9	10
11	12	13	14	15	16	17	18	19	20
21	22	23	24	25	26	27	28	29	30
31	32	33	34	35	36	37	38	39	40
41	42	43	44	45	46	47	48	49	50
51	52	53	54	55	56	57	58	59	60
61	62	63	64	65	66	67	68	69	70
71	72	73	74	75	76	77	78	79	80
81	82	83	84	85	86	87	88	89	90
91	92	93	94	95	96	97	98	99	100

Colour these numbers red: 45 86 12
Now subtract 10 from each of the numbers and colour the answer blue. For each one you should find that your blue square is above your red square.

Subtract 9 from each of the red numbers and colour the answer yellow.
Now subtract 11 from each of the red numbers and colour the answer green.
Look carefully at the patterns.

Find the answers to these questions.

52 - 9 =

40 - 11 =

63 - 9 =

64 - 9 =

52 - 11 =

15 - 11 =

78 - 9 =

71 - 9 =

46 - 9 =

81 - 11 =

32 - 11 =

27 - 11 =

I can...
I can add a set of one-digit and two-digit numbers together quickly. ☐
I can identify patterns and relationships involving subtraction of 9 or 11. ☐
I can subtract 9 from any two-digit number. ☐
I can subtract 11 from any two-digit number. ☐

Andrew Brodie: Number Journey for ages 7-8 © A&C Black Publishers Ltd 2008

Teacher's notes

Building on previous learning
Before starting this unit check that the children can already:
- use practical and informal written methods to add two-digit numbers
- recall addition facts for each number to 20
- recall sums of multiples of 10
- partition three-digit numbers into multiples of 100, 10 and 1

Learning objectives
- Develop and use written methods to record, support or explain addition of two-digit and three-digit numbers.

Learning outcomes
The children will be able to:
- partition two-digit numbers into multiples of 10 and 1 and use this to support their processing of addition.
- partition three-digit numbers into multiples of 100, 10 and 1 and use this to support their processing of addition.

Success criteria
Can the children…
… partition numbers into multiples of 10 and 1 to complete these questions: 51 + 36, 63 + 15, 45 + 24?
… partition numbers into multiples of 100, 10 and 1 to complete these questions: 265 + 131, 354 + 224, 421 + 163, 555 + 234, 516 + 38, 64 + 137?

Resources needed
- A clear school policy on the systems and methods to be used in recording additions both informally and formally. The method that we follow I this book is logical and is used by many schools. Your school will need to decide whether to use the terminology of either 'ones' or 'units' or both and whether to add the units first or the tens first in questions such as 63 + 42.

Opportunities for using and applying the skills
- Solving problems involving addition in the context of numbers or money.
- Identifying patterns and relationships involving numbers and using these to solve problems.

45

Developing and using written methods for the addition of two-digit and three-digit numbers

Help at home sheet

Child's name: **Date:**

Dear Parents

At school we follow the National Curriculum and the Primary Framework for mathematics. One aspect of our work in mathematics is the learning of number skills, including developing and using written methods for addition of two-digit and three-digit numbers. There are lots of methods that can be used for addition. The method that we are showing on this sheet may not be the method that you are most familiar with but it is very logical and provides a great start towards developing quicker methods later. We are keen to involve parents in their children's learning so you may like to help your child by using some of the ideas on this sheet.

National Curriculum

The Primary Framework for mathematics says that Year 3 pupils should:

• develop and use written methods to record, support or explain addition and subtraction of two-digit and three-digit numbers.

You could...

... practise additions with your child using the method outlined here of partitioning the numbers into hundreds, tens and units. (You could explain to your child that some people prefer to call the 'units' by the name 'ones'.) To find the answer to an addition question such as 53 + 46 we split it into the 3 units and 6 units and the 5 tens and 4 tens:

Write: $53 + 46 = (3 + 6) + (50 + 40) = 9 + 90 = 99$

To find the answer to an addition question such as 269 + 127 we split it into the 9 units and 7 units, the 6 tens and 2 tens and the 2 hundreds and 1 hundred:

Write: $269 + 127 = (9 + 7) + (60 + 20) + (200 + 100) = 16 + 80 + 300 = 396$

... practise these additions with your child using the partitioning method:

28 + 39 =	37 + 23 =	59 + 11 =
243 + 235 =	476 + 123 =	531 + 356 =

You may like to let us know how your child gets on with these activities – if so please return this sheet with any comments on the back.

Andrew Brodie: Number Journey for ages 7-8 © A&C Black Publishers Ltd 2008

Worksheet 1

Name: _____

Date: _____

On this page I am going to add two-digit numbers to two-digit numbers.

Look:

We use brackets to keep the units together.

$$42 + 36 = (2 + 6) + (40 + 30) = 8 + 70 = 78$$

We use brackets to keep the tens together.

Use the same method to answer these questions.

51 + 36 _____ =

63 + 15 _____ =

45 + 24 _____ =

74 + 32 _____ =

48 + 23 _____ =

56 + 17 _____ =

73 + 25 _____ =

74 + 25 _____ =

75 + 25 _____ =

Andrew Brodie: Number Journey for ages 7-8 © A&C Black Publishers Ltd 2008

Developing and using written methods for the addition of two-digit and three-digit numbers

Worksheet 2

Name: _____

Date: _____

Look:

We use brackets to keep the units together.

We use brackets to keep the tens together.

643 + 125 = (3 + 5) + (40 + 20) + (600 + 100) = 8 + 60 + 700 = 768

We use brackets to keep the hundreds together.

Use the same method to try these questions.

265 + 131 _____ =

354 + 224 _____ =

421 + 163 _____ =

555 + 234 _____ =

Look:

841 + 38 = (1 + 8) + (40 + 30) + 800 = 879

We didn't need brackets for the hundreds this time because 38 is only a two-digit number and doesn't have any hundreds.

Try these questions.

516 + 38 _____ =

64 + 137 _____ =

 I can...

I can add two-digit numbers together. ☐

I can add three-digit numbers together. ☐

I can add two-digit numbers to three-digit numbers. ☐

Efficient written methods for subtraction - complementary addition

Teacher's notes

Building on previous learning

Each school should have a clear policy decision regarding the approaches to written calculations. At this stage most schools will wish to build on their pupils' skills and knowledge in the use of number lines, possibly introducing subtraction by decomposition in Year 4. Before starting this unit check that the children can already:

- recall addition and subtraction facts for each number to 20.
- recall sums and differences of multiples of 10.
- partition three-digit numbers into multiples of 100, 10 and 1.

Learning objectives

- Develop and use written methods to record, support or explain subtraction of two-digit and three-digit numbers.

Learning outcomes

- The children will be able to subtract two-digit and three-digit whole numbers using the process of subtraction by complementary addition.

Success criteria

Can the children…

… subtract two-digit numbers from two-digit numbers: 91 - 53, 48 - 29, 54 - 36, 88 - 21, 65 - 32, 94 - 47, 73 - 35, 69 - 44?

… subtract three-digit numbers from multiples of 100: 800 - 590, 600 - 117, 700 - 439, 900 - 199, 500 - 264?

Resources needed

- A clear school policy on the systems and methods to be used in recording subtractions both informally and formally.
- A variety of number lines, including those marked with every number, those marked only in multiples of 10 and those marked only in multiples of 100. These can be used for demonstration purposes to remind the pupils of the processes that they are following and can also be accessed by pupils when they need to refer to them.

Opportunities for using and applying the skills

- Solving problems involving subtraction in the context of numbers or money.
  Identifying patterns and relationships involving numbers and using these to solve problems.
  For example, to find 67 - 42, the pupils will:

    start at 42 and jump forward 8 to 50   jump forward 10 to 60   jump forward 7 to 67

    30 31 32 33 34 35 36 37 38 39 40 41 42 43 44 45 46 47 48 49 50 51 52 53 54 55 56 57 58 59 60 61 62 63 64 65 66 67 68 69 70

    Using their knowledge of adding strings of numbers together the pupils now add the three 'jumps':
    8 + 10 + 7 = 25   so   67 - 42 = 25

Andrew Brodie: Number Journey for ages 7-8 © A&C Black Publishers Ltd 2008

Efficient written methods for subtraction - complementary addition

Help at home sheet

Child's name: **Date:**

Dear Parents

At school we follow the National Curriculum and the Primary Framework for mathematics. One aspect of our work in mathematics is the learning of number skills, including developing and using written methods for subtraction of two-digit and three-digit numbers. There are lots of methods that can be used for subtraction. The method that we are showing on this sheet may not be the method that you are most familiar with but it is very logical and provides a great start towards developing quicker methods later. We are keen to involve parents in their children's learning so you may like to help your child by using some of the ideas on this sheet.

National Curriculum

The Primary Framework for mathematics says that Year 3 pupils should:

* develop and use written methods to record, support or explain addition and subtraction of two-digit and three-digit numbers.

You could...

… practise subtractions with your child using the method outlined here. First draw a simple number line, marked with the multiples of 10 from 0 to 100:

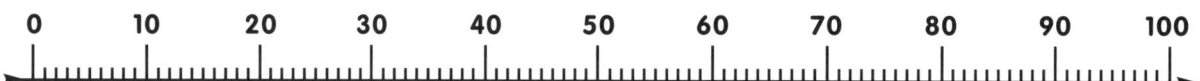

Start with subtractions such as 68 - 21 and use the number line to 'jump' from 21 to 30, then from 30 to 60, then from 60 to 68:

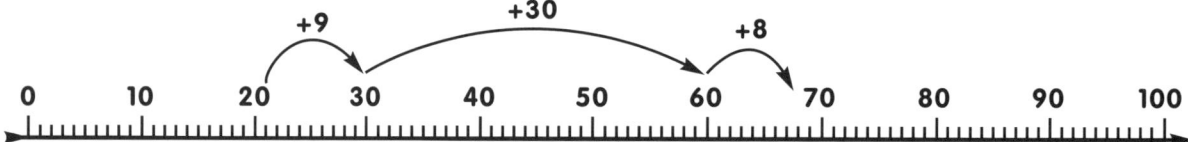

Now your child can add the jumps together to make 47:

    9 + 30 + 8 = 47   So   68 - 21 = 47

Practise lots of questions like these where each number has two digits. As your child becomes more confident he/she may not need to use the number line but will be able to make the 'jumps' in his/her head. Encourage your child to write down the maths systematically. The example above should be written like this:

    68 - 21   9 + 30 + 8 = 47   68 - 21 = 47

Here are some questions that can be answered in this way:

    49 - 17   53 - 24   62 - 29   81 - 46   95 - 78   100 - 52

You could ask your child to invent some of his/her own questions to work out.

You may like to let us know how your child gets on with these activities – if so please return this sheet with any comments on the back.

Andrew Brodie: Number Journey for ages 7-8 © A&C Black Publishers Ltd 2008

Efficient written methods for subtraction - complementary addition

Worksheet 1

Name: _____

Date: _____

0   10   20   30   40   50   60   70   80   90   100

On this page I will be subtracting two-digit numbers.

I want to subtract 34 from 89. 89 - 34 I can use the number line to help me.

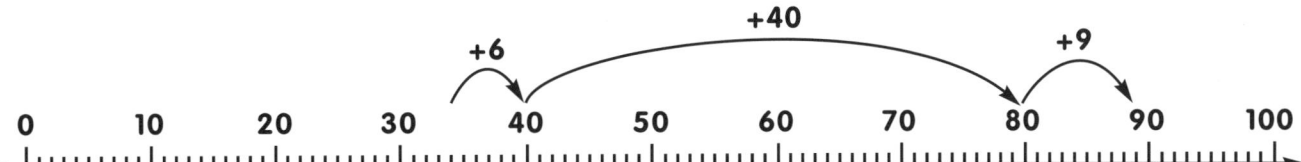

This is how I should lay out the question and its solution.

89 - 34	6 + 40 + 9 = 55	89 - 34 = 55

Try this method for answering the following questions.

91 - 53 _____

48 - 29 _____

54 - 36 _____

88 - 21 _____

65 - 32 _____

94 - 47 _____

73 - 35 _____

69 - 44 _____

Andrew Brodie: Number Journey for ages 7-8 © A&C Black Publishers Ltd 2008

Efficient written methods for subtraction - complementary addition

Name: _____

Date: _____

| 0 | 100 | 200 | 300 | 400 | 500 | 600 | 700 | 800 | 900 | 1000 |

I want to subtract 231 from 400. 400 - 231
I can use the number line to help me.

+9 +60 +100

| 0 | 100 | 200 | 300 | 400 | 500 | 600 | 700 | 800 | 900 | 1000 |

This is how I should lay out the question and its solution.

| 400 - 231 | 9 + 60 + 100 = 169 | 400 - 231 = 169 |

Try this method for answering the following questions.

800 - 590 _____

600 - 117 _____

700 - 439 _____

900 - 199 _____

500 - 264 _____

 I can...

I can subtract two-digit numbers. ☐
I can subtract three-digit numbers. ☐

Andrew Brodie: Number Journey for ages 7-8 © A&C Black Publishers Ltd 2008

Teacher's notes

Building on previous learning
Before starting this unit check that the children can already:
- derive and recall multiplication facts for the 2, 5 and 10 times-tables and the corresponding division facts

Learning objectives
- Derive multiplication facts for the three times-table.
- Recall multiplication facts for the three times-table.
- Derive the related division facts for the three times-table.
- Recall the related division facts for the three times-table.

Learning outcomes
The children will be able to:
- find the multiplication facts for the three times-table.
- recall the multiplication facts for the three times-table.
- find the division facts for the three times-table.
- recall the division facts for the three times-table.

Success criteria
Can the children…
… recall multiplication facts for the three times-table: 6 x 3, 8 x 3, 2 x 3, 10 x 3, 3 x 3, 9 x 3, 1 x 3, 5 x 3?
… recall division facts for the three times-table: 18 ÷ 3, 12 ÷ 3, 6 ÷ 3, 21 ÷ 3, 24 ÷ 3, 15 ÷ 2, 27 ÷ 3, 30 ÷ 3?

Resources needed
- A number line from 0 to 100.
- A display of the three times-table. Note that we are using the traditional layout of the three times-table, e.g. '4 x 3 = 12' to represent four threes are twelve. Some schools may prefer to choose to write four threes are twelve as '3 x 4 = 12'.

Opportunities for using and applying the skills
- Solving problems involving addition, subtraction, multiplication and division in the context of numbers or money.
- Identifying and recording the information and calculation needed to solve a problem; carrying out the calculations and checking the solutions.
- Describing patterns and relationships involving numbers.
- Presenting information in lists, tables and simple diagrams.

53

Multiplication facts for the three times-table, and related division facts

Help at home sheet

Child's name: **Date:**

Dear Parents

At school we follow the National Curriculum and the Primary Framework for mathematics. One aspect of our work in mathematics is the learning of number skills, including learning the three times multiplication table and the division facts that arise from it. We are keen to involve parents in their children's learning so you may like to help your child by using some of the ideas on this sheet.

National Curriculum

The Primary Framework for mathematics says that Year 3 pupils should:

• derive and recall multiplication facts for the 3 times-table and the corresponding division facts.

You could...

... practise the 3 times-table every day for a week – in the car, when walking, last thing at night before bedtime, first thing in the morning. It is important on each occasion to keep the practice short, perhaps just one or two minutes. Let your child read the table below. With plenty of practice you will find that he/she hardly needs to refer to it at all.

1 x 3 = 3	one times three is three
2 x 3 = 6	two threes are six
3 x 3 = 9	three threes are nine
4 x 3 = 12	four threes are twelve
5 x 3 = 15	five threes are fifteen
6 x 3 = 18	six threes are eighteen
7 x 3 = 21	seven threes are twenty-one
8 x 3 = 24	eight threes are twenty-four
9 x 3 = 27	nine threes are twenty-seven
10 x 3 = 30	ten threes are thirty

Once you feel that your child is confident with saying the table, ask individual questions such as: 'What's five times three?' 'Six threes?' 'Eight multiplied by three?'

If you feel that your child is able to answer the multiplication questions easily, try some division questions: 'How many threes make twenty-one?' 'Divide eighteen by three.'

You may like to let us know how your child gets on with these activities – if so please return this sheet with any comments on the back.

Andrew Brodie: Number Journey for ages 7-8 © A&C Black Publishers Ltd 2008

Multiplication facts for the three times-table, and related division facts

Worksheet 1

Name: _____

Date: _____

On this page I am going to make the three times-table.

Draw rings around the triangles to make groups of three.

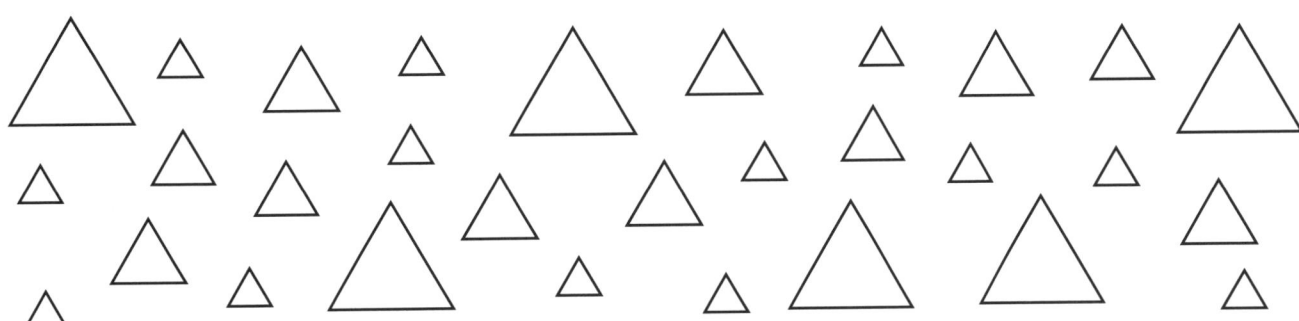

Write the three times-table.

1 x 3 = [ ]   one times three is _____

2 x 3 = [ ]   two threes are _____

3 x 3 = [ ]   three threes are _____

4 x 3 = [ ]   four threes are _____

5 x 3 = [ ]   five threes are _____

6 x 3 = [ ]   six threes are _____

7 x 3 = [ ]   seven threes are _____

8 x 3 = [ ]   eight threes are _____

9 x 3 = [ ]   nine threes are _____

10 x 3 = [ ]   ten threes are _____

Look at this multiplication fact: $8 \times 3 = 24$

We can use this fact to find two division facts: $24 \div 3 = 8$ and $24 \div 8 = 3$

Multiplication facts for the three times-table, and related division facts

Worksheet 2

Name: _____

Date: _____

Look at the three times-table. Write division facts next to the multiplication facts. The first four have been done for you.

1 x 3 = 3	3 ÷ 3 = 1	3 ÷ 1 = 3
2 x 3 = 6	6 ÷ 3 = 2	6 ÷ 2 = 3
3 x 3 = 9	_____	There is only one division fact for this one.
4 x 3 = 12	_____	_____
5 x 3 = 15	_____	_____
6 x 3 = 18	_____	_____
7 x 3 = 21	_____	_____
8 x 3 = 24	_____	_____
9 x 3 = 27	_____	_____
10 x 3 = 30	_____	_____

fold here

Fold the paper so that you can't see the three times-table!

Can you answer these questions quickly without looking at the table?

6 x 3 = ☐	8 x 3 = ☐	2 x 3 = ☐	10 x 3 = ☐
18 ÷ 3 = ☐	12 ÷ 3 = ☐	6 ÷ 3 = ☐	21 ÷ 3 = ☐
3 x 3 = ☐	9 x 3 = ☐	1 x 3 = ☐	5 x 3 = ☐
24 ÷ 3 = ☐	15 ÷ 2 = ☐	27 ÷ 3 = ☐	30 ÷ 3 = ☐

 I can...

I can remember the multiplication facts for the three times-table ☐
I can remember the division facts for the three times-table. ☐

56

Andrew Brodie: Number Journey for ages 7-8 © A&C Black Publishers Ltd 2008

Multiplication facts for the four times-table, and related division facts

Teacher's notes

Building on previous learning
Before starting this unit check that the children can already:
- derive and recall multiplication facts for the 2, 5 and 10 times-tables and the corresponding division facts

Learning objectives
- Derive multiplication facts for the four times-table.
- Recall multiplication facts for the four times-table.
- Derive the related division facts for the four times-table.
- Recall the related division facts for the four times-table.

Learning outcomes
The children will be able to:
- find the multiplication facts for the four times-table.
- recall the multiplication facts for the four times-table.
- find the division facts for the four times-table.
- recall the division facts for the four times-table.

Success criteria
Can the children…
… recall multiplication facts for the four times-table: 6 x 4, 9 x 4, 3 x 4, 10 x 4, 7 x 4, 2 x 4, 4 x 4, 8 x 4?
… recall division facts for the four times-table: 40 ÷ 4, 24 ÷ 4, 4 ÷ 4, 16 ÷ 4, 36 ÷ 4, 12 ÷ 4, 28 ÷ 4, 32 ÷ 4?

Resources needed
- A number line from 0 to 100
- A display of the four times-table. Note that we are using the traditional layout of the four times-table, e.g. '3 x 4 = 12' to represent three fours are twelve. Some schools may prefer to choose to write three fours are twelve as '4 x 3 = 12'.

Opportunities for using and applying the skills
- Solving problems involving addition, subtraction, multiplication and division in the context of numbers or money.
- Identifying and recording the information and calculation needed to solve a problem; carrying out the calculations and checking the solutions.
- Describing patterns and relationships involving numbers.
- Presenting information in lists, tables and simple diagrams.

Multiplication facts for the four times-table, and related division facts

Help at home sheet

Child's name: **Date:**

Dear Parents

At school we follow the National Curriculum and the Primary Framework for mathematics. One aspect of our work in mathematics is the learning of number skills, including learning the four times multiplication table and the division facts that arise from it. We are keen to involve parents in their children's learning so you may like to help your child by using some of the ideas on this sheet.

National Curriculum

The Primary Framework for mathematics says that Year 3 pupils should:
• derive and recall multiplication facts for the 4 times-table and the corresponding division facts.

You could...

... practise the four times-table every day for a week – in the car, when walking, last thing at night before bedtime, first thing in the morning. It's important on each occasion to keep the practice short, perhaps just one or two minutes. Let your child read the table below. With plenty of practice you will find that he/she hardly needs to refer to it at all.

$1 \times 4 = 4$	one times four is four
$2 \times 4 = 8$	two fours are eight
$3 \times 4 = 12$	three fours are twelve
$4 \times 4 = 16$	four fours are sixteen
$5 \times 4 = 20$	five fours are twenty
$6 \times 4 = 24$	six fours are twenty-four
$7 \times 4 = 28$	seven fours are twenty-eight
$8 \times 4 = 32$	eight fours are thirty-two
$9 \times 4 = 36$	nine fours are thirty-six
$10 \times 4 = 40$	ten fours are forty

Once you feel that your child is confident with saying the table, ask individual questions such as: 'What's six times four?' 'Three fours?' 'Seven multiplied by four?'

If you feel that your child is able to answer the multiplication questions easily, try some division questions: 'How many fours make thirty-two?' 'Divide twenty by four.'

You may like to let us know how your child gets on with these activities – if so please return this sheet with any comments on the back.

Andrew Brodie: Number Journey for ages 7-8 © A&C Black Publishers Ltd 2008

Multiplication facts for the four times-table, and related division facts

Worksheet 1

Name: _____

Date: _____

On this page I am going to make the four times-table.

Draw rings around the squares to make groups of four.

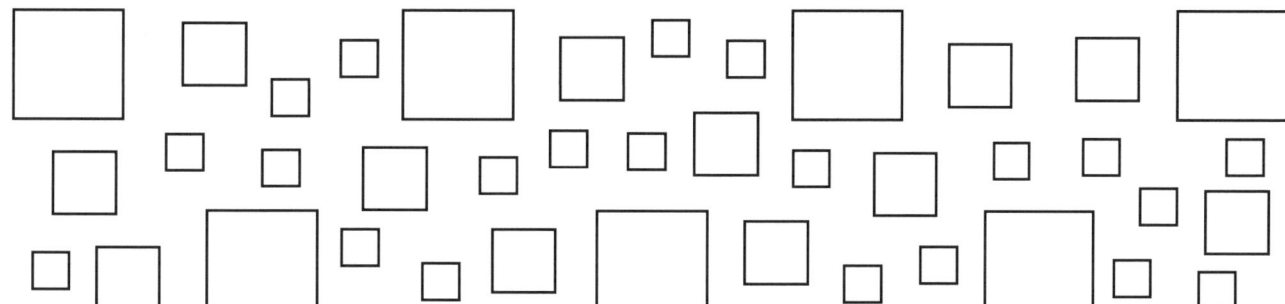

Write the four times-table.

1 x 4 = [ ]   one times four is _____

2 x 4 = [ ]   two fours are _____

3 x 4 = [ ]   three fours are_____

4 x 4 = [ ]   four fours are_____

5 x 4 = [ ]   five fours are _____

6 x 4 = [ ]   six fours are _____

7 x 4 = [ ]   seven fours are _____

8 x 4 = [ ]   eight fours are _____

9 x 4 = [ ]   nine fours are _____

10 x 4 = [ ]   ten fours are _____

Look at this multiplication fact: 7 x 4 = 28

We can use this fact to find two division facts: 28 ÷ 4 = 7 and 28 ÷ 7 = 4

Andrew Brodie: Number Journey for ages 7-8 © A&C Black Publishers Ltd 2008

Multiplication facts for the four times-table, and related division facts

Worksheet 2

Name: _____

Date: _____

Look at the four times-table. Write division facts next to the multiplication facts. The first four have been done for you.

1 x 4 = 4   4 ÷ 4 = 1   4 ÷ 1 = 4

2 x 4 = 8   8 ÷ 4 = 2   8 ÷ 2 = 4

3 x 4 = 12   _____   _____

4 x 4 = 16   _____

                                       There is only one division fact for this one.

5 x 4 = 20   _____   _____

6 x 4 = 24   _____   _____

7 x 4 = 28   _____   _____

8 x 4 = 32   _____   _____

9 x 4 = 36   _____   _____

10 x 4 = 40   _____   _____

fold here

- -

Fold the paper so that you can't see the four times-table!

Can you answer these questions quickly without looking at the table?

6 x 4 = ☐   9 x 4 = ☐   3 x 4 = ☐   10 x 4 = ☐

40 ÷ 4 = ☐   24 ÷ 4 = ☐   4 ÷ 4 = ☐   16 ÷ 4 = ☐

7 x 4 = ☐   2 x 4 = ☐   4 x 4 = ☐   8 x 4 = ☐

36 ÷ 4 = ☐   12 ÷ 4 = ☐   28 ÷ 4 = ☐   32 ÷ 4 = ☐

 **I can...**   I can remember the multiplication facts for the four times-table. ☐

I can remember the division facts for the four times-table. ☐

Andrew Brodie: Number Journey for ages 7-8 © A&C Black Publishers Ltd 2008

Multiplication facts for the six times-table, and related division facts

Teacher's notes

Building on previous learning
Before starting this unit check that the children can already:
- derive and recall multiplication facts for the 2, 5 and 10 times-tables and the corresponding division facts

Learning objectives
- Derive multiplication facts for the six times-table.
- Recall multiplication facts for the six times-table.
- Derive the related division facts for the six times-table.
- Recall the related division facts for the six times-table.

Learning outcomes
The children will be able to:
- find the multiplication facts for the six times-table.
- recall the multiplication facts for the six times-table.
- find the division facts for the six times-table.
- recall the division facts for the six times-table.

Success criteria
Can the children…
… recall multiplication facts for the six times-table: 4 x 6, 9 x 6, 1 x 6, 3 x 6, 5 x 6, 7 x 6, 2 x 6, 8 x 6?
recall division facts for the six times-table: 48 ÷ 6, 24 ÷ 6, 18 ÷ 6, 42 ÷ 6, 60 ÷ 6, 30 ÷ 6, 54 ÷ 6, 12 ÷ 6?

Resources needed
- A number line from 0 to 100.
- A display of the six times-table. Note that we are using the traditional layout of the six times-table, e.g. '8 x 6 = 48' to represent eight sixes are forty-eight. Some schools may prefer to choose to write eight sixes are forty-eight as '6 x 8 = 48'.

Opportunities for using and applying the skills
- Solving problems involving addition, subtraction, multiplication and division in the context of numbers or money.
- Identifying and recording the information and calculation needed to solve a problem; carrying out the calculations and checking the solutions.
- Describing patterns and relationships involving numbers.
- Presenting information in lists, tables and simple diagrams.

Multiplication facts for the six times-table, and related division facts

Help at home sheet

Child's name: **Date:**

Dear Parents

At school we follow the National Curriculum and the Primary Framework for mathematics. One aspect of our work in mathematics is the learning of number skills, including learning the six times-table and the division facts that arise from it. We are keen to involve parents in their children's learning so you may like to help your child by using some of the ideas on this sheet.

National Curriculum

The Primary Framework for mathematics says that Year 3 pupils should:
- derive and recall multiplication facts for the six times-table and the corresponding division facts.

You could...

... practise the six times-table every day for a week – in the car, when walking, last thing at night before bedtime, first thing in the morning. It's important on each occasion to keep the practice short, perhaps just one or two minutes. Let your child read the table below. With plenty of practice you will find that he/she hardly needs to refer to it at all.

$1 \times 6 = 6$	one times six is six
$2 \times 6 = 12$	two sixes are twelve
$3 \times 6 = 18$	three sixes are eighteen
$4 \times 6 = 24$	four sixes are twenty-four
$5 \times 6 = 30$	five sixes are thirty
$6 \times 6 = 36$	six sixes are thirty-six
$7 \times 6 = 42$	seven sixes are forty-two
$8 \times 6 = 48$	eight sixes are forty-eight
$9 \times 6 = 54$	nine sixes are fifty-four
$10 \times 6 = 60$	ten sixes are sixty

Once you feel that your child is confident with saying the table, ask individual questions such as: 'What's seven times six?' 'Three sixes?' 'Five multiplied by six?'

If you feel that your child is able to answer the multiplication questions easily, try some division questions: 'How many sixes make thirty?' 'Divide forty-two by six.'

You may like to let us know how your child gets on with these activities – if so please return this sheet with any comments on the back.

Andrew Brodie: Number Journey for ages 7-8 © A&C Black Publishers Ltd 2008

Multiplication facts for the six times-table, and related division facts

Worksheet 1

Name: _____

Date: _____

On this page I am going to make the six times-table.

Draw rings around the hexagons to make groups of six.

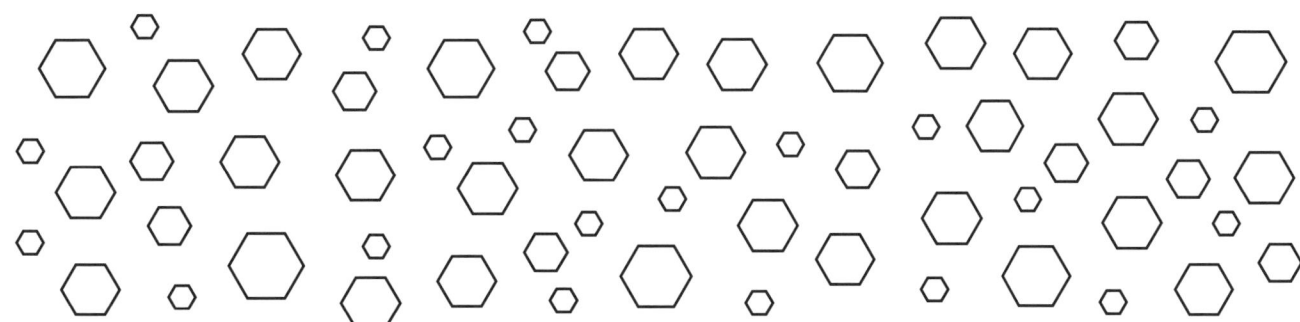

Write the six times-table.

1 x 6 = [ ]   one times six is _____

2 x 6 = [ ]   two sixes are _____

3 x 6 = [ ]   three sixes are _____

4 x 6 = [ ]   four sixes are _____

5 x 6 = [ ]   five sixes are _____

6 x 6 = [ ]   six sixes are _____

7 x 6 = [ ]   seven sixes are _____

8 x 6 = [ ]   eight sixes are _____

9 x 6 = [ ]   nine sixes are _____

10 x 6 = [ ]   ten sixes are _____

Look at this multiplication fact: 9 x 6 = 54

We can use this fact to find two division facts: 54 ÷ 6 = 9 and 54 ÷ 9 = 6

Andrew Brodie: Number Journey for ages 7-8 © A&C Black Publishers Ltd 2008

Multiplication facts for the six times-table, and related division facts

Worksheet 2

Name: _____

Date: _____

Look at the six times-table. Write the division facts next to the multiplication facts. The first four have been done for you.

1 x 6 = 6	6 ÷ 6 = 1	6 ÷ 1 = 6
2 x 6 = 12	12 ÷ 6 = 2	12 ÷ 2 = 6
3 x 6 = 18	_____	_____
4 x 6 = 24	_____	_____
5 x 6 = 30	_____	_____
6 x 6 = 36	_____	There is only one division fact for this one.
7 x 6 = 42	_____	_____
8 x 6 = 48	_____	_____
9 x 6 = 54	_____	_____
10 x 6 = 60	_____	_____

fold here

Fold the paper so that you can't see the six times-table!

Can you answer these questions quickly without looking at the table?

4 x 6 = ☐	9 x 6 = ☐	1 x 6 = ☐	3 x 6 = ☐
48 ÷ 6 = ☐	24 ÷ 6 = ☐	18 ÷ 6 = ☐	42 ÷ 6 = ☐
5 x 6 = ☐	7 x 6 = ☐	2 x 6 = ☐	8 x 6 = ☐
60 ÷ 6 = ☐	30 ÷ 6 = ☐	54 ÷ 6 = ☐	12 ÷ 6 = ☐

I can remember the multiplication facts for the six times-table. ☐

I can remember the division facts for the six times-table. ☐

64

Andrew Brodie: Number Journey for ages 7-8 © A&C Black Publishers Ltd 2008